GOD'S FIVE CALLINGS
FOR EVERY MAN

*Discover How to be a Man, a Husband,
a Father, a Churchman and a Witness for God!*

DR. STEPHEN SWIHART

Scripture quotations are taken from the
HOLY BIBLE, NEW INTERNATIONAL VERSION.
Copyright © 1973, 1978, 1984
International Bible Society.
Used by permission of Zondervan Bible Publishers.

WWW.MASTERPLANMINISTRIES.COM
1333 El Reno Street
Elkhart, IN 46516
Email: steve@MasterPlanMinistries.com

Suggested Guidelines

Here are six short and specific guidelines that will help you get the most from these daily devotions.

1. First of all, decide right now that you will be everything God wants you to be. Determine in your heart of hearts that you will be a *real Christian* and *a spiritual man of God!*

2. Every day, before you open this book, get your heart ready. Pray for God to speak to you. Pray He will change you more and more into His own image. Pray He will help you fulfill the plans He has for you.

3. Read through each lesson *twice*. Take your time. This is not a race. Underline key ideas, and read them over and over until they sink deeply into your heart. Meditate. Soak.

4. When you answer the daily devotional questions, be transparent, humble and hungry to live in the exact center of God's will.

5. Go through this book with someone else. Ask someone to join you in this exercise. Then, *every day* call each other for a short period of accountability and prayer. Help one another grow stronger in the Lord. *(This suggestion is usually the one that produces the greatest benefit.)*

6. Finally, when you finish this book, ask the Lord this question: *Is there another man You want me to take through this devotional book so he will experience the five callings You have for him?* Never stop helping fellow men until everyone has been reached!

Contents

Calling Number One:
What It Means to be a Man of God
Page 7

Calling Number Two:
What It Means to be a Husband for God
Page 33

Calling Number Three:
What It Means to be a Father for God
Page 65

Calling Number Four:
What It Means to be a Churchman for God
Page 91

Calling Number Five:
What It Means to be a Witness for God
Page 117

What it Means to be
A MAN OF GOD

WEEK ONE - Day 1

The Critical Starting Point

No one is born "a man of God." Instead, men of God are made one at a time.

There are many "beginnings" in life: the beginning of infancy, the beginning of school, the beginning of marriage, and so on. There is another "beginning" that outweighs all of the others in importance. This is the time when you begin to be a MAN OF GOD.

Most men never experience this unique beginning. They may claim to believe in God, and they may attend church or live a generally moral life, but these things are not the same as being a true MAN OF GOD.

So, how can a person get started on this unique journey? How can someone truly begin to be a MAN OF GOD? According to the Bible, this is the starting line: *the fear of the Lord.* Proud men do not fear God or prepare for judgment; they cannot imagine that they are going to be punished for their actions. But they are wrong. Everyone will someday be judged by God, and spiritual men prepare for it.

Men who fear God have a profound respect for His perfections and a deep shame for their own imperfections. What about you? Have you started this special journey?

A Personal Application

Closely examine Proverbs 1:7 and Romans 1:18-32. Explain why wise men fear God.

_____
_____
_____
_____
_____
_____
_____
_____
_____
_____
_____
_____
_____
_____
_____
_____
_____

WEEK ONE - Day 2

Fear and Forgiveness

Men of the world may conquer outer space, but men of God master inner space — the heart.

When everything is said and done, there are only two types of men: those who fear the Lord's judgments, and those who give little-to-no thought about their personal judgments before a holy God.

The first group of men can point to a time when they humbled themselves before the Judge and asked for complete forgiveness for all of the inappropriate things they have ever done. As a result of this humble action, all of the men in this group received God's full pardon and started their journey as MEN OF GOD.

The second group of men cannot find any such turning point in their past, and if they can, they know they have long since walked away from it. The men in this grouping are MEN OF THE WORLD. They do not love God, but themselves, their jobs, their possessions, and their pleasures.

What about yourself? Is your forgiveness and fear up to date? Is your spiritual experience fresh and alive?

A Personal Application

Slowly read 2 Corinthians 5:11-21, and explain "the message of reconciliation."

_____
_____
_____
_____
_____
_____
_____
_____
_____
_____
_____
_____
_____
_____
_____
_____
_____
_____

WEEK ONE - Day 3

God Owes You Nothing

The best of men are but men at the best
- Thomas Brooks.

Genuine MEN OF GOD have a wholesome fear of God because they have taken the time to examine their own hearts with complete honesty. They know that they have no room to boast about their character. They fall short in their attitudes and actions every day, and they know it. MEN OF GOD are acutely aware of the fact that God owes them nothing. Therefore, they do not boast about their self-inflated goodness, but about God's amazing grace.

When men compare themselves with other men, they usually come out above average. But when they compare themselves with God's Ten Commandments, they can see that they are guilty of breaking every one of them! They have no defense. They are guilty, and they admit it.

While MEN OF GOD understand that they deserve hell because of their many sins, they are remarkably confident of going to heaven because of the forgiveness they have received from their Savior, Jesus Christ. They never take this unprecedented love for granted. It is forever branded in their hearts that they have the privilege to love Him only because He first loved them!

A Personal Application

Patiently examine the Ten Commandments in Exodus 20:1-20. How does God's standard differ from man's standard?

_____
_____
_____
_____
_____
_____
_____
_____
_____
_____
_____
_____
_____
_____
_____
_____
_____
_____

WEEK ONE - Day 4

Weighing Sin's Consequences

There are only two great motivators in life — love and fear.

The thought of having to leave your home and go overseas to fight in a major war should generate a measure of fear in anyone's heart. On the other hand, the thought of an all-out war, with thundering bombs, rumbling tanks, and enemy soldiers coming to your own neighborhood is considerably more frightening!

But there is another fear — a far more grave one — that should outweigh the threat of war: *the fear that you will have to face God someday and receive an everlasting judgment that is based on His standards, not your motives!*

The MAN OF GOD knows that this is a big deal because the consequences of pride and presumption could mean not only a verdict of "Guilty," but an endless sentence in hell! This is not something he takes lightly.

Pause and think for a moment. Is your relationship with God motivated in a wholesome way by the fear of sin's consequences?

For the rest of your life, remember the following two major facts: The man who fears God, has nothing else to fear. But the man who treats God halfheartedly has everything to fear!

A Personal Application

Thoughtfully read Luke 12:4-10 and Philippians 2:12. How can you apply this teaching about fear?

WEEK ONE - Day 5

The Best Kind of Success

Significant successes in life are never automatic; they are reserved for men who fear the Lord.

MEN OF GOD do not obey Him and the Scriptures because it is easy or because it is fun. They obey God and His Word because it is the right thing to do!

More than that, MEN OF GOD also know that wholesome fear and obedience to God and the Bible will produce incredible success stories like these: the forgiveness of every sin, peace of mind, undefeatable hope, practical discernment, wise money management, rewarding relationships, sound decisions, integrity, prosperity and more! God always rewards pure hearts!

MEN OF GOD also understand that disobedience to the Lord and His Word is the soil that produces these kinds of weeds: separation from God's favor, dysfunctional relationships, family turmoil, depression, lack of money, loss of respect, and a thousand other headaches and heartaches. So before they act impulsively, MEN OF GOD count the cost; they consider the consequences of their actions.

All men want to succeed in life. But only those who are willing to fear and obey God will taste the best kind of success.

A Personal Application

Based on Deuteronomy 6:1-9, what are the essential keys to success?

_____
_____
_____
_____
_____
_____
_____
_____
_____
_____
_____
_____
_____
_____
_____
_____
_____
_____
_____
_____

WEEK ONE - Days 6-7

Thinking It Through

Take two days to review the previous five lessons. Write out a prayer that reflects what you desire to apply from these lessons.

WEEK TWO - Day 1

A Foundation of Obedience

*In the beginning you make
your own decisions,
later your decisions make you!*

Just as surely as a man can build a house or a business or a particular skill, so a man can build his faith and his obedience to God. MEN OF GOD are not flawless in anything they do, but they are determined to grow in their faithfulness to God in order that they might become the men, husbands, fathers, churchmen and witness that God intends.

Most men take a measure of pride in their character, but MEN OF GOD place their greatest pride in Christ. They respect him because of his impeccable integrity, and they follow him because of his practical wisdom. They are also prepared to lay down their lives for Christ, because they know that he laid down his own life for them.

Ask any man of the world if it is wise to follow his own heart, and he will tell you "Yes." Ask any MAN OF GOD the same question, and he will tell you "No." Real MEN OF GOD try their best to follow God's heart (not their own), and that means they are soundly committed to obeying the teachings found in the Holy Bible.

Is this how your family and friends view you?

A Personal Application

When you read Matthew 7:21-27, what do you hear the Lord Jesus saying to you about the nature of a Godly man?

_____
_____
_____
_____
_____
_____
_____
_____
_____
_____
_____
_____
_____
_____
_____
_____
_____
_____

WEEK TWO - Day 2

"Believer" or Obedient Man of God?

"Believers" are a dime a dozen; genuine "men of God" are priceless.

Any coward can say in his heart that he "believes" in God. But it takes a real MAN OF GOD to step up to the plate and follow Jesus Christ 24/7, in private and in public. Many men "think" they believe in God, many men "attend" church occasionally, and many men "try" to be good, but very few men are authentic MEN OF GOD.

According to the Bible, only those men who gladly die to their own will and wholeheartedly follow God's will are the real deal. The rest are phonies at worst or superficial at best.

Slowly work your way through the following list. What is the truthful answer to each question?

- Who controls your *time*, Christ or yourself?
- Who controls your *money*, Christ or yourself?
- Who controls your *decisions*, Christ or yourself?

Do you need to pray more about finding and following God's will moment by moment? If so, why not start *right away*?

A Personal Application

What can you learn from Luke 14:25-35 about a lifestyle of obedience?

WEEK TWO - Day 3

The Heart of Every Man's Problems

Every man suffers from an inner corruption until Christ takes control of his heart.

MEN OF GOD know who they are at their core, and they are not proud of their past inconsistencies, misaligned priorities, neglect of the Bible and prayer, mishandled relationships, lack of holiness, and the like. They know all too well that man's boastings about his possessions, power and pleasures are horribly superficial. They want more. (Please read this important paragraph one more time.)

MEN OF GOD, above everything else, want a new heart. They are not content with the status quo. **They want to be different, and they know that at the heart of all their problems is the problem of their very own heart!** So, they look to heaven, and they ask God to change them from the inside-out so they can live a lifestyle of love and obedience.

No man can stand tall until he has first bent low. The way to spiritual success is not found in following the crowd, but in following the Lord. The backbone of all victory is loving obedience to God's will. The MAN OF GOD has no other ambition.

Is this your testimony?

A Personal Application

Prayerfully read and underline the key thoughts in Psalm 51. What does the Lord want you to experience from these words?

_____
_____
_____
_____
_____
_____
_____
_____
_____
_____
_____
_____
_____
_____
_____
_____
_____
_____

WEEK TWO - Day 4

Choosing Between Fun and Favor

*Shallow men do whatever they want to do.
Mature men do whatever God wants them to do.*

There are many choices in life, but the only one that interests the MAN OF GOD is the one with this mark: "Obedience to God's Will."

The devil would like nothing more than for you to think for yourself, to decide for yourself, and to make up your own mind about this and that. So he dangles every sort of deception and enticement in front of you in order to get you to follow his own will. But regardless of how much "popularity" or "fun" a worldly decision may seem to offer, the MAN OF GOD will have nothing to do with it. He is not interested in worldly *fun*, but in Divine *favor*. He lives for the glory of God, not for frivolous entertainment.

Surely Christian men want to enjoy life like everyone else, but not at the expense of disobeying God. So they turn off foul television shows, they refuse to rent unwholesome movies, they do not waste money gambling, they protect their eyes from corrupt internet sites, and so on. They soundly reject worldly *fun* because they have discovered far greater benefits in pursuing God's *favor*!

A Personal Application

Identify at least three things in 1 Peter 1:13-20 that you will pray about today.

WEEK TWO - Day 5

Overcoming Disobedience

When water is only 99% pure, the remaining 1% will probably make you sick.

It has often been said that you cannot keep birds from flying over your head, but you *can* keep them from building a nest in your hair. In a similar way, you cannot prevent every temptation from entering your mind, but you *can* decide early on that you will not give any temptation lodging in your life! MEN OF GOD are tempted like everyone else, and sometimes they fall short and sin, but what distinguishes them from other men is this: *they hurt when they sin, and they take whatever steps are required to make matters right after they fail.*

- How well do you guard your eyes?
- How well do you guard your ears?
- How well do you guard your feet?
- How well do you guard your relationships?
- How well do you assume responsibility for your own faults?

If you are struggling with obedience to God's will in any area of your life, admit it and get help *today!* Call your pastor or a friend or a Christian counselor. Don't put it off. Make purity your top priority!

Here's another tip: Everyone needs a purity-partner. Who holds *you* accountable and helps to keep you clean?

A Personal Application

Rewrite the essence of Ephesians 4:17-32 in your own words. Make it both practical and personal.

WEEK TWO - Days 6-7

Thinking It Through

Take two days to review the previous five lessons. Write out a prayer that reflects what you desire to apply from these lessons.

WEEK THREE - Day 1

First Love

When the bottom line is drawn, God doesn't want your help or money — He wants your heart.

There are a whopping 613 laws from God in the first five books of the Bible. That's a lot of law! But in the books of the New Testament there are at least 621 imperatives we are expected to follow — that's even a larger number of commandments!

It would be easy to look at all of these rules and conclude that God and the Bible are only interested in a bunch of meaningless do's and don'ts. But that would be a gross mistake. In reality, all of the laws in God's Book are *love*-laws; they actually explain the proper way we are to love God and people. Without these rules, we'd be left to follow only our easily misguided emotions. So, God helps us love in a better way by showing us His own *love*-rules. Now, that puts a whole new perspective on the Bible and the Lord's commands, doesn't it?

Say it over to yourself, again and again: *At the heart of the Bible, and at the heart of a MAN OF GOD is love. Vertical love — love for God. And horizontal love — love for people. Therefore, I will make it my objective to learn God's Word more and more so I can love better and better!*

A Personal Application

Read Mark 12:28-34, and write out two ways you can improve your love for God and your love for people.

_____
_____
_____
_____
_____
_____
_____
_____
_____
_____
_____
_____
_____
_____
_____
_____
_____

WEEK THREE - Day 2

Losing Your First Love

Theological correctness is no substitute for a pure and passionate love.

You have probably seen artificial fireplaces. They look real. In fact, the imitation fire sometimes seems so real that you have to get very close before you can detect that the flames are fake. The same thing can be true when a man loses his first love for God. Outwardly, at a distance, he may seem to love the Lord. He may attend church, believe the Bible, put his money in the offering plate, sing in the choir, and hold a church office (maybe even be the pastor!). But when you look closer, you notice the fire — the first love — is not real; it is more mechanical than meaningful.

When a MAN OF GOD loses his first love for the Lord, he simply goes through the motions of being loving. His heart really isn't in it. He may do any number of good works, but on the inside he knows he's largely faking it. The love that is in his heart is not deep, but shallow. When this happens, there is just one cure for a decline in first love: *repentance*. The heart must be set ablaze again, and only the Lord can do that.

Let's be honest today, have you lost your first love for the Lord? If this describes you, take your time and ask the Lord for a love-renewal. If your heart is where it should be, ask the Lord to help you keep it there.

A Personal Application

What does the Lord have to say about a loss of "first love" in Revelation 2:1-7? Write out a prayer in response to this important passage.

_____
_____
_____
_____
_____
_____
_____
_____
_____
_____
_____
_____
_____
_____
_____
_____
_____
_____
_____
_____

WEEK THREE - Day 3

Priorities

Your priorities will make you . . . or break you!

It isn't enough to be *sincere;* God expects you to be *spiritual*. MEN OF GOD know what it is to talk the talk, but they hunger to walk the walk every day and everywhere.

This means that spiritual men work hard at keeping minor things minor in their list of priorities while keeping major things major. For them, their relationship with God is their uppermost priority. Next, comes their wife, followed by their children. Then, comes work.

In order for a man (or anyone) to be truly spiritual, each day must begin and end with time spent in God's presence. MEN OF GOD make it a priority to set aside time for daily prayer and Bible study. Sure, they will miss doing this now and then, but this will be the exception to the rule.

When you understand how important it is to have a meaningful connection with God every day, you will keep this appointment as your top priority. MEN OF GOD know they need more of God in their lives, so they adjust their schedules in order to keep Him both first in their *lives* and first in their *day*. They are passionate about being more than *good;* they long to be *Godly*.

A Personal Application

Read Philippians 3:1-17 slowly. Write out a personal prayer based on this passage.

WEEK THREE - Day 4

Meaningful Prayer

Stop going to prayer; start going to God!

When you pray, do not focus on prayer, but on God. Praying, by itself, is worthless. But actually connecting with God is priceless. Make it your goal to come into God's presence every time you pray. Here are some things you can do to improve your prayer times.

1. Ask the Lord to teach you how to pray. Tell Him you are willing to take months (even years) to learn this most important discipline.

2. Look at the prayers in the Bible; learn to pray from other significant MEN OF GOD (Psalm 9, 51, 119; Matthew 6:9-13; Luke 22:39-42; Acts 4:23-31; Ephesians 1:15-23; 3:14-21; Colossians 1:9-14; etc.).

3. Read books on prayer. Consider volumes by Andrew Murray, E. M. Bounds, David Y. Cho, and many others.

4. Pray with others who know how to pray. Listen for discernment and faith.

5. Just do it!

A Personal Application

Pray these words from Psalm 119:9-30. What do you find here that you need to add to your own prayers?

_____
_____
_____
_____
_____
_____
_____
_____
_____
_____
_____
_____
_____
_____
_____
_____
_____
_____
_____
_____

WEEK THREE - Day 5

Meaningful Bible Reading

Do not go to the Bible for answers; go to God's Word for anointing!

Every time you read your Bible you should hear the voice of God speaking to you. If that doesn't happen, you are reading too quickly and without a sufficiently open heart. Here are some tips for more effective Bible reading.

1. Read through whole books of the Bible. Begin with short ones, like Philippians, 1 & 2 Timothy, Titus, James, 1 John, and so on.

2. Don't rush your reading. Take your time. Think of Bible devotions as a *prayer* exercise. Ask God to highlight special words and phrases and verses just for you. Listen for God's voice speaking to you as you read His Word.

3. Read with understanding. Consult Bible commentaries and dictionaries when passages are unclear. (If you do not have one, develop your own Christian library of reference materials.)

4. Make *personal transformation* your goal, not merely the completion of a reading assignment. Read to meet God; read to change into His image.

A Personal Application

Pray-read Psalm 19:7-14. Write out what God is saying to you from these verses.

_____
_____
_____
_____
_____
_____
_____
_____
_____
_____
_____
_____
_____
_____
_____
_____
_____

WEEK THREE - Days 6-7

Thinking It Through

Take two days to review the previous five lessons. Write out a prayer that reflects what you desire to apply from these lessons.

WEEK FOUR - Day 1

Partners

The ultimate success of every man depends on the quality of his relationships.

Every man needs a safety net — that is, he needs another man (or a small group of men) who will be quick to pray both *for* him and *with* him. Men need *partners!*

Imagine this; ten times the great apostle Paul requested prayer from others (Romans 15:30-31; Ephesians 6:19-20; Colossians 4:2-4; etc.). He didn't try to live the Christian life by himself. Instead, he relied on the prayers of others to help him. You and I must do the same thing.

The Christian life is not designed to be lived alone, with only faith and willpower to get you through your days. Instead, the spiritual life is a team-enterprise, it is a joint-effort. God intends for no man to be an island, but an interlocking piece in the jig-saw puzzle called "life." So . . .

- For whom do you pray daily?
- Who prays for you daily?

If you are not connected with another man on a prayer level, you need to ask the Lord for such a friend *this week*. Whom will you contact?

A Personal Application

Read Colossians 4:2-4 and 4:12-13. Prepare a list of reasons why it would be wise for you to have a prayer-partner.

WEEK FOUR - Day 2

Choosing the Right Friends

It's a simple rule: good friends will make you better; bad friends will make you worse.

A good friend will agree with you when you are right, and he will correct you when you are wrong. He will listen sympathetically when you hurt, and he will be there whenever you need help. But more than anything else, *a good friend will consistently try to guide you into God's will for your life.* Without any doubt, your most valuable assets in life will always be *holy* friends.

On the other hand, your worst liabilities will always be poor relationships. Bad friends are more likely to get you into trouble than out of it. Poor career associates are more likely to create problems than peace. And superficial "harmless friends" are more likely to make you worldly than Godly.

Of all the decisions you will make in a lifetime, who you choose to be your closest friends will largely determine the amount of wisdom and joy you will experience. Therefore, mature MEN OF GOD surround themselves with the most respected, holy and loyal men they can find.

Take a quick survey of your friends. Are they interested in your total wellbeing: spirit, soul, and body?

A Personal Application

How do the following passages describe a good friend? See Proverbs 17:17; 27:17 and Ecclesiastes 4:12.

_____
_____
_____
_____
_____
_____
_____
_____
_____
_____
_____
_____
_____
_____
_____
_____
_____
_____
_____
_____

WEEK FOUR - Day 3

Peer Pressure

Every man of God will be confronted with this choice: should I follow the crowd or should I follow Christ?

Peer pressure is as old as time itself — in the very beginning Eve enticed Adam to eat from the forbidden tree, and he chose to follow her into sin rather than to follow God's will and enjoy the best in life. Adam fell to peer pressure, and most people have been doing the same thing ever since.

On more than a few occasions you will be encouraged by some associate to listen to a dirty joke, watch an immoral movie, abuse your body with some drug, take the Lord's name in vain, steal an employer's property, misrepresent the truth, and so on. There is no limit to the number of ways people can "twist your arm" to do something inappropriate.

MEN OF GOD choose their fear — and they choose to fear God, not people. They will not follow the crowd when it would be wrong to do so. Instead, they go against the grain, and they do what is right, even when it isn't popular.

How do you handle peer pressure? How good are you at saying "No" to temptations from "friends?"

A Personal Application

Read Psalm 1 slowly. Underline key words and phrases. Based on this passage, how can you defeat peer pressure?

_____
_____
_____
_____
_____
_____
_____
_____
_____
_____
_____
_____
_____
_____
_____
_____
_____
_____
_____
_____

WEEK FOUR - Day 4

More Than A Teaching

A man who can see God will never see an unsolvable problem.

Everyone knows that life is full of problems, and some of these difficulties can be *really* big. The MAN OF GOD is not immune to these sorts of trials. He experiences them like everyone else, but he is different from others in this way: *he is able to trust God to get him through all of his ordeals!*

It is one thing to agree with the *teaching* that God can get you through anything; it is another matter altogether to possess a personal *testimony* of how God has helped you through your trials! Right?

God is searching for men who want more than a *teaching*. He is looking for men who are willing to trust Him with their problems so He can give them a *testimony* of His power, love and faithfulness!

When you trust God for literally *everything,* you will soon find He is capable of giving you two things: (1) the *miracles* you need *to remove* nasty ordeals from your life, and (2) the *grace* you need *to go through* the remaining ordeals He wants to use to make you more mature.

Either way — miracle or grace — MEN OF GOD possess testimonies of His help!

A Personal Application

Read 2 Corinthians 12:6-10. Explain how this story can help you with your own ordeals.

_____
_____
_____
_____
_____
_____
_____
_____
_____
_____
_____
_____
_____
_____
_____
_____
_____
_____

WEEK FOUR - Day 5

Responding with Faith

Before you let your problems get you down, let God's promises lift you up.

Here is a critical fact of life that every MAN OF GOD needs to recognize: *My problems cannot defeat me; only I can defeat me!*

Honestly, your problems are never the real problem. Instead, how you choose to *respond* to your problems is always the decisive issue. Say it out loud: *My problems cannot defeat me if I will respond to them the way God wants!*

- Today, practice verbalizing what you see in the *Word* and not what you see in the *world*.

- Today, practice *trusting* God with *everything*.

When you train your heart and tongue to trust God with your problems, He will trust you with His promises! (Read this sentence one or two more times.)

Set aside three times today to reread this page slowly. Pray each time that God will help you to see your trials as He sees them. Record the times when you do this:

❏ _____ ❏ _____ ❏ _____

A Personal Application

Slowly and prayerfully read Romans 8:28-39. Underline the most important words and phrases. Lastly, write out a prayer asking God to help you confront all of your problems with a strong faith.

_____
_____
_____
_____
_____
_____
_____
_____
_____
_____
_____
_____
_____
_____
_____
_____
_____

WEEK FOUR - Days 6-7

Thinking It Through

Take two days to review the previous five lessons. Write out a prayer that reflects what you desire to apply from these lessons.

What it Means to be
A HUSBAND FOR GOD

WEEK FIVE - Day 1

The Starting Line

Any man can become a husband, but you must determine to become more — a husband who leads his wife by God's Word!

When you decide deep inside your heart that you will be a genuine MAN OF GOD, you are laying the foundation for the next calling on your life — to be a true HUSBAND FOR GOD.

The uniting of a man and a woman in marriage is the most significant institution in all of society because it is intended to reflect that ultimate union that will take place between Jesus Christ (the Groom) and his Church (the Bride). Therefore, marriage should not be entered into with only sincerity, but with spirituality and a full knowledge of God's plans for its design.

In all honesty, many men are not prepared for marriage when the pastor says, "You may kiss the bride." There may be good intentions and warm feelings at that moment, but most men know very little about what it means to be a HUSBAND FOR GOD. However, men can learn what God expects from them as husbands. And when they do, they can create a relationship with their spouse that is spiritually strong and mutually fulfilling for a lifetime!

Are you eager to become the husband God intends for you to be?

A Personal Application

Read Ephesians 5:31-33.
Write out two practical ways you can apply this passage to your marriage.

_____
_____
_____
_____
_____
_____
_____
_____
_____
_____
_____
_____
_____
_____
_____
_____
_____
_____
_____
_____

WEEK FIVE - Day 2

Pastoring Your Wife (1)

Your wife needs you to be her full-time pastor.

The instant you say, "I do" at the marriage altar, God pronounces you the *pastor* of your wife. You may have a great pastor in your *church,* but when it comes to your *home,* you are to be the great pastor there. As the pastor of your wife, there are several things God expects from you. Here is the first one.

Right out of the box the Lord (and your wife) expects you to talk the talk and to walk the walk of what it means to be a Godly man. There is no substitute for being your wife's role model. She should always look up to you and regard you with the greatest respect because she knows it is your highest desire to reflect God's own character.

Any husband can be *average,* but the HUSBAND FOR GOD detests lukewarmness. He lives to be the man, the husband, the father, the churchman and the witness God made him to be. He is not interested in minimal standards and fuzzy commitments. He intends to be the real deal. He wants to *be* want God wants him to be, and he wants to *say* what God wants him to say, and he wants to *do* whatever God wants him to do!

This is the backbone of a solid, spiritual marriage. Ask God to make you into the husband He wants you to be.

A Personal Application

Closely examine Ephesians 5:25-30. How does the Lord expect you to love your wife?

_____
_____
_____
_____
_____
_____
_____
_____
_____
_____
_____
_____
_____
_____
_____
_____
_____
_____
_____
_____
_____
_____
_____

WEEK FIVE - Day 3

Pastoring Your Wife (2)

Building a spiritual marriage is more important than building a mansion!

There is much more to being a true HUSBAND FOR GOD than going to work, paying the bills and remaining sexually faithful. As the pastor of your wife, "you must know the condition of your flock" (Proverbs 27:23). That is, you must know the spiritual health of your wife: her level of faith, her degree of obedience, her consistency in Bible reading and prayer, her struggles with sin, and the like. In short, it is your first duty as a HUSBAND FOR GOD to help your wife become as spiritual a woman as she can be.

The apostle Paul tells us that Jesus gave up his life for us so that through his works and through the teachings of the Bible we could become clean, spotless, glorious, without a single spot or wrinkle or blemish. Then Paul develops an unexpected application. He states that husbands, like Christ, are to lay down their own lives and devote themselves to the purification of their wives through God's Word. In other words, as HUSBANDS FOR GOD, we men are to see to it that our wives become and remain spiritually radiant. We are to wash our wives with the Word until they sparkle!

Do you wash your wife?

A Personal Application

Patiently look again at Ephesians 5:25-33. Based on these verses, identify at least three ways you can love your wife like Christ.

_____
_____
_____
_____
_____
_____
_____
_____
_____
_____
_____
_____
_____
_____
_____
_____
_____
_____
_____

WEEK FIVE - Day 4

Pastoring Your Wife (3)

Only sin can keep a couple from God, and only God can keep a couple from sin.

Sooner or later, every marriage runs into trouble: anger, disappointment, inappropriate speech, misplaced priorities, lack of communication, and the like. During these moments it is critical to understand that the largest problem in every man's home can be reduced to a single word: SIN. And the essence of sin can be reduced to the single letter between the "S" and the "N." The "I"-life is the rub. This happens when the "I" turns into self-centeredness, self-pity, self-justification, self-madeness, and the like.

When your marriage hits a bump (and it will more than once!), it's imperative that *you* take the initiative to heal the wounds. As the pastor of your wife, you need to pray for her, love her, and lead her back to the center of God's will. Of course, you begin this process by getting your own act together before God.

As a HUSBAND FOR GOD you must make every effort to see that both you and your wife consistently put the Lord first in your lives. Above everything else, you should desire to have a holy marriage that is based on spiritual priorities. Is this the kind of marriage you are seeking to develop?

A Personal Application

Read Galatians 5:16-26. Explain the difference between being controlled by your sinful nature and being filled with the Holy Spirit.

_____
_____
_____
_____
_____
_____
_____
_____
_____
_____
_____
_____
_____
_____
_____
_____
_____
_____
_____

WEEK FIVE - Day 5

Protecting Your Wife

In order to protect your marriage and home you must detect and defeat all the worldliness that wants to invade it.

The deepest problems in marriage will always be spiritual in nature, therefore the HUSBAND FOR GOD intentionally aims first and foremost to be a holy example for his wife. Then, he works to help his wife be holy as well. This means he will do everything he can to see to it that his wife is not only a Christian, but a woman who desires strongly to live her life in the very center of God's will. The true HUSBAND FOR GOD wants to be strong in the Lord, and he desires for his spouse to be strong, too.

Godly husbands know that the worldliness of the world can subtly slip into their homes. For instance, through their jobs, personal friends, television shows, rented movies, the internet, music preferences, and the like, Christian values can be compromised. So the HUSBAND FOR GOD works diligently both to guard his wife and to train her in spiritual discernment. He sees to it that nothing is permitted to enter his home that will threaten to weaken their walk with the Lord.

Are you intentionally protecting yourself and your wife from subtle worldliness?

A Personal Application

After you read Colossians 2:8; 3:1-11, and 1 John 2:15-17, explain at least three ways these verses can be applied in your own home.

_____
_____
_____
_____
_____
_____
_____
_____
_____
_____
_____
_____
_____
_____
_____
_____
_____
_____
_____

WEEK FIVE - Days 6-7

Thinking It Through

Take two days to review the previous five lessons. Write out a prayer that reflects what you desire to apply from these lessons.

WEEK SIX - Day 1

Loving Your Wife

Love is not about what you get, but about what you give.

Unfortunately, a large number of people have a misunderstanding of the true nature of love. We often define love as a strong *feeling* that we have in our hearts for someone, but this idea is foreign to the Bible. Instead of locating love in our *emotions*, the deepest level of love is actually found in our *will*.

When you love your wife with only your *emotions*, you can only show your affection for her when you *feel* love. But when you love her with your *will*, you can show your love for her whether or not there are any feelings present. In other words, love is not a feeling-based *noun*, but a serving-based *verb*. **Real love does the right thing even when there are no feelings to back up the action!**

This kind of love is at the heart of the wedding vows: *for better for worse, for richer for poorer, in sickness and in health . . . till death do we part.* At one time you probably said these words (or similar ones). Now, when you practice these words, you are displaying the true essence of love.

Remember, HUSBANDS FOR GOD do not promise to love their wives as long as loving feelings are present, but even if they are absent. That's love! (Read this entire lesson a second time.)

A Personal Application

What a difference there would be in our homes if we practiced 1 Corinthians 13. Read this chapter, then identify any attitudes, words or actions you need to replace with love.

_____
_____
_____
_____
_____
_____
_____
_____
_____
_____
_____
_____
_____
_____
_____
_____
_____
_____
_____

WEEK SIX - Day 2

Praying for Your Wife

At the beginning and ending of every day you should pray for your wife.

Your wife needs your love, but she has another need that is even greater: *she needs an awareness of the presence of God in her life!* She desires that *you* will be with her through the trials and triumphs of her life, and she longs to sense that *God* is with her every step of the way as well.

When you pray for your wife, ask Him to do more than simply "bless" her. Here are some other ideas to add to your praying:

- Pray she will know what it means to walk with God every day.

- Pray she will gladly and profitably maintain a strong habit of reading God's Word daily.

- Pray she will enjoy intimacy with the Lord through prayer.

- Pray she will become and remain truly strong in the Lord.

- Pray she will be literally used by God both inside and outside your home.

HUSBANDS FOR GOD long to see their spouses live as WIVES FOR GOD.

A Personal Application

What can you find in these prayers from the apostle Paul to help you pray more effectively for your wife? See Ephesians 1:15-23 and Colossians 1:9-14.

WEEK SIX - Day 3

Providing for Your Wife

Every husband should find practical ways to make his wife happy and effective.

The HUSBAND FOR GOD has more than *spiritual* duties; he has numerous practical *physical* obligations as well. Therefore, he will work diligently to meet the nitty-gritty demands of daily life at home, too.

- This means he will find a job and work hard in order to provide shelter, food, clothing and medicine for his household. He will always want his wife to feel secure and safe.

- This means he will maintain his house well. What needs fixing will be fixed, what needs painting will be painted, what needs replaced will be replaced, and so on.

- This means he will see that all of the appliances in the home are in good working order.

- This means he will help with household chores, especially if his wife works outside of the home. He will gladly help clean the house, do the laundry, cook the meals and wash the dishes.

Right?!

A Personal Application

Based on 1 Peter 3:7, think of several specific ways you can help your wife and keep from hindering your own prayer life.

_____
_____
_____
_____
_____
_____
_____
_____
_____
_____
_____
_____
_____
_____
_____
_____
_____
_____
_____

WEEK SIX - Day 4

When Problems Arise (1)

God has a simple formula for marriage success: apply His Word day after day.

The main difference between a home that comes through a storm and a home that collapses within the storm is this: *the foundation.* Husbands who build their homes on the foundation of God's Word will manage to get through their ordeals. But husbands who build their households principally on personal preferences and good intentions will usually have a much tougher time.

Listen carefully. It isn't enough to be a Christian husband. It isn't enough to attend church. And it isn't enough to believe the Bible. Thousands upon thousands of married couples have claimed all of these things and still failed miserably. Why? Here are three possibilities: (1) Not everyone who says he is a Christian actually is one. (2) Not everyone who attends church goes there to become stronger in the Lord. And (3), not everyone who *believes* the Bible really *obeys* the Bible.

Solid-rock marriages are not the by-product of husbands and wives who *appreciate* God's Word, but who actually *apply* it to themselves!

Is *obeying* God's Word the top priority in your home?

A Personal Application

Look closely at Matthew 7:24-27. How solid is the foundation in your home. Are there any areas that need some repairs? Be specific.

_____
_____
_____
_____
_____
_____
_____
_____
_____
_____
_____
_____
_____
_____
_____
_____
_____
_____

WEEK SIX - Day 5

When Problems Arise (2)

Success in marriage is not so much about agreeing with each other as it is about agreeing with God.

Envision a pyramid in your mind. Place your name at the lower left corner of the triangle. Put your wife's name at the opposite (lower right) corner. On this chart you and your spouse are as far apart as you can get. So, how can you get closer together without moving to the left or to the right?

Here's the answer. Write the word "Bible" at the top of the pyramid. Now, as a husband, climb up your side of the triangle toward the top. Go as far as you can go every day and every night. Then pray and encourage your wife to do the same thing on her side of the triangle. Notice what happens as each of you pursue God and His will for your lives. *Not only do you make personal progress in your spiritual pilgrimage, you also grow closer to each other as you get closer to obeying the Scriptures!*

All husband-wife problems are first husband-God and/or wife-God problems. In other words, if there are *horizontal marital difficulties,* you can be certain that these trials are the by-product of prior *vertical spiritual problems.* Make it your daily ambition to live close to God, then you will have the foundation for living close to your spouse!

A Personal Application

Meditate on James 1:19-26. Identify two or three main points for a personal and marital application.

_____
_____
_____
_____
_____
_____
_____
_____
_____
_____
_____
_____
_____
_____
_____
_____
_____
_____
_____
_____

WEEK SIX - Days 6-7

Thinking It Through

Take two days to review the previous five lessons. Write out a prayer that reflects what you desire to apply from these lessons.

WEEK SEVEN - Day 1

Date Your Mate

Small, regular and sincere displays of affection can transform your marriage.

When a man spends more time thinking about his job, his car, his house, his TV and his hobbies than his wife, his marriage is in trouble.

HUSBANDS FOR GOD do not take their wives for granted. Neither do they give them just a sliver of their time and attention. They do more. They spend ample time with them. *They often date their mate.*

You should never stop "dating" your wife. That is, you should continue getting together and spending time enjoying each other. There are a million ways you can do this: eating out, going for an extended drive in the country, taking a weekend retreat to a popular area, attending a marriage seminar, walking slowly through novelty shops together, enjoying a private picnic, setting aside one night a week for dessert and communication, going to bed at the same time and talking for a good twenty minutes, and so on.

Husbands, here's a valuable tip: *take the lead and make dating your wife a fixed part of your schedule.* Write it on the calendar. Treat your wife to a regular and special date!

A Personal Application

What words do you find in Philippians 2:1-11 that can help you love your wife more?

_____
_____
_____
_____
_____
_____
_____
_____
_____
_____
_____
_____
_____
_____
_____
_____
_____
_____
_____
_____
_____
_____

WEEK SEVEN - Day 2

Communication

A good marriage requires good communication.

The success of any marriage is directly connected to the level of enjoyment husbands and wives share in communicating with each other. When talking and listening is strong, the marriage will be healthy. But when communication is strained, the relationship will be weak. Perhaps more than any other area, men often need to improve their communication skills.

How well do you listen to your wife? Do you hear what she is *saying* and *feeling?* Do you give her plenty of time to share everything that's on her mind? Do you convey genuine interest?

Likewise, husbands, do you tell your wife everything that's inside your own chest? Do you "bottle up" your own thoughts and feelings, or are you transparent and honest? Are you really able to "connect" with your wife verbally?

If communication is a strength in your marriage, congratulations. But if it needs some improvement, don't put it off. Talk to each other about your talking. Work on it. If you need help, by all means get it!

A Personal Application

Study closely Ephesians 4:29-5:2. Think of at least two things you should do in the light of these verses.

_____
_____
_____
_____
_____
_____
_____
_____
_____
_____
_____
_____
_____
_____
_____
_____
_____
_____
_____
_____
_____
_____

WEEK SEVEN - Day 3

Finances (1)

Whenever your outgo exceeds your income, then your upkeep will become your downfall
— Anonymous.

According to family counselors, the number one cause for conflicts in the home is money problems. Usually that means there isn't enough money. And often that means there is some kind of failure in money management that needs to be addressed.

When finances are a sore spot in any marriage, the first matter that must be examined is the budget. Make a list of all your household's monthly income after taxes. Put that amount at the top of a clean sheet of paper.

Next, make a list of all the family expenses for a month. Consult your check register and bank statements for accuracy. Remember to add in all of the "loose" money you spend from your pocket or purse. Include *everything*.

Finally, subtract your expenses from your income (assuming that's possible). This figure should tell you how much money you actually have leftover every month. Now, resolve as a family to get out of debt! Unity is essential. Make temporary sacrifices in order to achieve family financial freedom. This is square one.

A Personal Application

Learning the secret of contentment is an important starting point in managing your finances. How can Philippians 4:10-13 help?

_____
_____
_____
_____
_____
_____
_____
_____
_____
_____
_____
_____
_____
_____
_____
_____
_____

WEEK SEVEN - Day 4

Finances (2)

If you have chronic financial problems, get money management counseling right away.

Whenever there is a financial problem in your home, this is what you must do: *increase* your income, and/or *decrease* your expenses.

You can increase your income by (1) getting a better paying job, (2) taking on a part-time job, and (3) selling items you have that you can't afford or don't need.

You can decrease your expenses by closely examining your budget and determining what you really don't *need* right now. You may *want* this or that, but if your plan is to get your money under control, then you must limit your spending habits for the time being. Make a list of *all* the things you can do to cut your expenses.

Next, pay off your smaller debts as quickly as possible. Then, apply this monthly sum to reduce your next debt until it is paid off.

Finally, cut your credit cards in half and throw them away. As much as possible, refuse to buy anything but your home and car on credit.

If you need more help, see your pastor or a financial counselor as soon as possible.

A Personal Application

There is no better cure for financial stress than faith in God's promises. Read Matthew 6:19-34, and record what God wants you to do?

_____
_____
_____
_____
_____
_____
_____
_____
_____
_____
_____
_____
_____
_____
_____
_____
_____
_____

WEEK SEVEN - Day 5

Choose People over Things

*Treasure things worth treasuring—
keep a tight hold on people;
keep a loose hold on things!*

Edmund Burke wrote, "What shadows we are, and what shadows we pursue." In other words, human beings are terribly temporal and superficial creatures. Worse yet, we are often inclined to devote our whole lives to things that are temporal and shallow.

It has been said, if it were possible to place everything in the whole world in a man's heart, he would still be missing something and want more. HUSBANDS FOR GOD understand this common deficiency in humans, so they decide that in their own hearts and homes there will be plenty of room for the two things that do last and have significance: a relationship with God and close bonds with people.

God made people to be connected to other people, not things. Good friends are a family's greatest asset. The more true friends you have, the richer you are. Make it your ambition to love people and to be loved by people. This is the sweetest perfume in all of life!

A Personal Application

Based on *Ecclesiastes* 4:9-12 and *Proverbs* 17:17, why are close friendships so important? Do you have close friends?

_____
_____
_____
_____
_____
_____
_____
_____
_____
_____
_____
_____
_____
_____
_____
_____
_____
_____
_____
_____
_____
_____

WEEK SEVEN - Days 6-7

Thinking It Through

Take two days to review the previous five lessons. Write out a prayer that reflects what you desire to apply from these lessons.

WEEK EIGHT - Day 1

Teamwork (1)

Families, by definition, are supposed to be a united team, a virtual dream team.

When a house is divided, it will eventually be destroyed from within. There simply cannot be three agendas in a healthy home: the husband's agenda, the wife's agenda, and the children's agenda.

Some families operate in a near state of constant chaos because everyone expects to get their own way all of the time. They have minimal *family*-orientation. Instead, everyone thinks the family is supposed to make *them* happy. This is simply wrong and counter-productive.

When homes are nothing more than hotels with a cafeteria and laundry facility, you no longer have a *family* — what you have are *independent individuals* sharing the same space.

HUSBANDS FOR GOD must become the master planners for their families. And this means they must get everyone in the home to operate from the same "play book." Independent agendas must be eliminated, and whole-family agendas must be established.

Men, how are you doing at *family* planning?

A Personal Application

Read Genesis 2:18-24 and Matthew 12:25. How can you apply these verses to the unity in your own home?

_____
_____
_____
_____
_____
_____
_____
_____
_____
_____
_____
_____
_____
_____
_____
_____

WEEK EIGHT - Day 2

Teamwork (2)

Some couples need to slow down and get to know one another heart-to-heart.

In many homes couples have forgotten how to be a *family*. Instead, they are hotels with a restaurant, laundry and shuttle service. Men, as the primary leader in your homes, you can do better than that.

Imagine what it would be like if you and your wife patiently sat down together for meals every day. Imagine what it would be like if you had regular spiritual discussions. Imagine what it would be like if you and your spouse worked together like a team.

- Are you and your wife moving in the same direction?
- Is there too much busyness in your home?
- Do you have ample times for significant communication?
- Are your personal preferences flexible? Does your wife possess the same flexibility?
- Do you pray and talk about family agendas?
- How would you feel if Jesus wanted to visit your home every evening for an hour or so?

A Personal Application

What needs to happen in order to see Philippians 4:4-9 become the primary atmosphere in your home? Be specific.

_____
_____
_____
_____
_____
_____
_____
_____
_____
_____
_____
_____
_____
_____
_____
_____
_____
_____
_____
_____

WEEK EIGHT - Day 3

Make Right Decisions

The difference between a "good" decision and a "great" decision is learning what most pleases God.

When it comes to making decisions, the real issue is not limited to *what* you want to do, but *why* you want to do it. The instant you do anything for any reason other than for the glory of God, you are moving in the wrong direction.

For example, you shouldn't buy things just because you want them or because you can afford them. You should buy things because you sense God's permission to make the purchase.

In a similar way, you shouldn't get involved in extended commitments just because you or your wife wants to participate in something. You should discuss your schedules with the Lord and with each other first. Not everything that is *good* is necessarily *best* for you or for the family.

Make the kinds of decisions that will avoid strife and promote unity. Think of how your wife will feel before you make a decision based on how you will feel. Work together. Practice seeing everything through the eyes of your spouse and your Lord.

A Personal Application

Identify at least three principles you can find about making good decisions based on these verses: 1 Corinthians 10:31; Ephesians 5:10 and Colossians 1:9-10.

_____
_____
_____
_____
_____
_____
_____
_____
_____
_____
_____
_____
_____
_____
_____
_____
_____
_____
_____

WEEK EIGHT - Day 4

Go to the Right Church

A lukewarm church will rarely make a family hot for God — it takes a special church to do that. Find it!

Some churches are better for your spiritual health than others. In fact, some churches are actually detrimental to your soul's wellbeing. Look closely at the following questions. Test the effectiveness of your church.

- Does your church believe in the full inspiration and authority of the Bible?

- Does your church teach the Bible in-depth?

- Does your church have small groups where you can develop intimate and rewarding friendships?

- Does your church have ministries that make a significant and positive impact on husbands and wives?

- Is your church literally fulfilling the Great Commission?

It isn't enough simply to go to church. You and your wife must go together to the *right* church.

A Personal Application

What can you discover about the right church in Matthew 28:19-20 and Revelation 3:14-22. Are you attending the right church?

_____
_____
_____
_____
_____
_____
_____
_____
_____
_____
_____
_____
_____
_____
_____
_____
_____
_____
_____
_____
_____

WEEK EIGHT - Day 5

Serving Your Church

Give your best to the right church, and it will pay you back.

The church does not exist solely to serve you. Rather, it exists to train you so you can become skillful and effective in serving others. The typical tradition of coming, sitting, singing, listening, giving and leaving does not reflect God's plan for His church. Instead, the Lord wants to *equip* you at church so you can literally learn how to make a difference in other people's lives.

When only 20% of the church's members do 80% of the church's work, there is a problem. But you and your wife can become part of the solution. Either individually or working together, you and your wife can become significant assets in your congregation.

The Lord Jesus Christ came to earth to create His Church. He loved it so much that He willingly died for it. Now, He is searching for men and women with a similar heart who will labor at His side to make the local church effective in reaching and transforming countless lives. He is looking for husbands and wives who will give themselves sacrificially in order to impact others. Have you joined His team?

A Personal Application

Slowly read through Ephesians 4:11-16. What is the main job of church leaders? And what is the main duty of church members?

_____
_____
_____
_____
_____
_____
_____
_____
_____
_____
_____
_____
_____
_____
_____
_____
_____
_____

WEEK EIGHT - Days 6-7

Thinking It Through

Take two days to review the previous five lessons. Write out two personal applications you want to keep based on this information. Also write out a prayer.

WEEK NINE - Day 1

Martha Versus Mary Service

Christian work can either empty you or fill you up — it all depends on your focus.

In the story of Martha and Mary in the Bible, there are some critical insights that will help each husband and wife as they seek to serve their church.

First, notice Martha. She wanted to serve the Lord, but she was worried about all the details that were involved in preparing a big meal for Him and his disciples. She even complained to Jesus that her sister wasn't helping. This is a classic case where the *work* of the Lord dominated her heart.

Second, observe Mary. She sat at Jesus' feet listening to his every word. Even Jesus refused to tell her to help her sister because she had chosen to do the better thing. This is a classic case where the *Lord* of the work dominated her heart.

Husbands, beware that you and your wife do not fall into the trap of putting the *work* of the Lord before the *Lord* of the work! Keep your focus on Jesus, not on the things you do for Him.

A Personal Application

Based on Luke 10:38-42, identify the traits of poor and good works for Christ. How can you apply this passage?

_____
_____
_____
_____
_____
_____
_____
_____
_____
_____
_____
_____
_____
_____
_____
_____
_____
_____
_____
_____
_____
_____

WEEK NINE - Day 2

Headship

Husbands, not wives, are responsible for the quality control of their households.

When God measures the operation and effectiveness of a home, the bulk of His attention goes to the husband. Why? Because he is the main person God holds responsible for a family's success. He is the "head" of the home, like a corporate president is the "head" of a business.

Husbands and wives may divide and share family chores in any number of ways, but when the bottom line is drawn, it is the husband who is ultimately responsible for everything that goes on in the house. For instance, he may not write out the checks for the monthly bills, but he is responsible to oversee the family finances. He may not personally be able to pray with the children every night, but he sees that it is done by someone. He may not be up to date on fashions, but he keeps his family well clothed. And so on.

Husbands, are you the leader in your home? Do you assume ultimate responsibility for every decision? Is your wife respectful of your authority?

If you need counsel in this area of your marriage, get it. Talk with some wise husbands; get their advice.

A Personal Application

In our modern culture we have virtually lost the concept of headship. What does 1 Corinthians 11:2-12 say about this subject that Christians need to hear today?

_____
_____
_____
_____
_____
_____
_____
_____
_____
_____
_____
_____
_____
_____
_____
_____

WEEK NINE - Day 3

Keep Your Marriage Fresh

Keep putting logs on the fire of your marriage!

Some marriages are like old clothes: faded and frayed — they caught your eye when they were new, but now they go almost unnoticed. HUSBANDS FOR GOD will see to it that that never happens in their marriage!

In order to keep your marriage fresh and interesting, like homemade bread from the oven that is served with a cup of hot chocolate, you'll need to work at it. Here are a few ideas.

(1) From time to time, break away from the routine of doing the same thing the same way every day — be creative and change the pattern for a while. (2) Do something interesting you've never done before. (3) Write a love letter to each other on every holiday and birthday. (4) Take on a project that you can accomplish together that promises to be fun. (5) Buy each other a simple love-gift every Friday for a month. (6) Take fifteen minutes to hold hands at least three times a week. (7) Work together to help someone with a need. Etcetera.

Don't let your marriage get in a rut. Fill it with surprises and fresh expressions of love. Work on it.

A Personal Application

Notice how the Lord leads David in Psalm 23. How can you bring a freshness to your leadership in your home?

_____
_____
_____
_____
_____
_____
_____
_____
_____
_____
_____
_____
_____
_____
_____
_____
_____
_____
_____

WEEK NINE - Day 4

Pray Together

Every husband needs a prayer partner — especially a wife who can agree with him.

The calling to be a HUSBAND FOR GOD is not a light one. It requires large amounts of love, patience, discernment, wisdom and energy to do it right.

While HUSBANDS FOR GOD try to be good in everything they do, they sometimes fail — their words and decisions can miss the mark. When that happens, they need to be restored both vertically (before God) and horizontally (before their wife). And the best way to do that is to make amends: assume responsibility for the consequences, apologize humbly, and pray together.

Of course, there are many times when husbands and wives should seek the Lord together over countless other issues: the purchase of an expensive item, a change in careers, needs they know about in other people, programs at the church, and so on. Holding hands and praying is a powerful way to bless others, and to bless your own marriage at the same time. Husbands and wives who do this well will erect a protective shield around themselves. More than that, they will enjoy special prosperity because they have learned how to trust God with everything.

Do you pray often with your spouse?

A Personal Application

When husbands and wives put on the full armor of God and pray, they can conquer the strongest trial that will come against them. Read Ephesians 6:10-18, and explain in specific detail what this means.

_____
_____
_____
_____
_____
_____
_____
_____
_____
_____
_____
_____
_____
_____
_____
_____
_____
_____

WEEK NINE - Day 5

Every Man's Five Callings

You are well on your way, but three more callings remain in your journey as a man.

When the Lord saves a man from the consequences of his sins, He places five progressive callings on his life.

First, he is called to be a MAN OF GOD, a man who is preeminently and joyfully committed to God's agenda twenty-four hours a day, in private and in public.

Second, he is called to be a HUSBAND FOR GOD. This is a man who assumes the role of being his wife's pastor for life.

Third, he is called to be a FATHER FOR GOD. Again, in this role he works diligently to be the primary pastor of his children — overseeing their personal salvation and spiritual development.

Fourth, he is called to be a CHURCHMAN FOR GOD. In this capacity he pursues spiritual training so he can serve the Lord and his church effectively.

Fifth, he is called to be a WITNESS FOR GOD. As the Lord's own ambassador, he prepares himself so he can skillfully lead people to Christ and salvation.

A Personal Application

Anyone who follows hard after God will have both companions and critics. Based on Joshua 24:14-24, how should you press on in your journey?

_____
_____
_____
_____
_____
_____
_____
_____
_____
_____
_____
_____
_____
_____
_____
_____
_____
_____

WEEK NINE - Days 6-7

Thinking It Through

Take two days to review the previous five lessons. Write out a prayer that reflects what you desire to apply from these lessons.

What it Means to be
A FATHER FOR GOD

WEEK TEN - Day 1

Pastoring Your Children (1)

Every child desperately needs a full-time pastor!

Any man can become the parent of children, but the FATHER FOR GOD knows that he must be more — he must also be their *pastor*.

A pastor (or shepherd) is someone who watches closely and cares wisely for the total wellbeing of his congregation. He is deeply interested in their spiritual, psychological, social and physical health. In the same way, as a FATHER FOR GOD, you are required to be thoroughly interested and involved in the multifaceted development of all your children.

Your kids need to learn how to be forgiven, how to pray, how to understand the Bible, and how to live for the glory of God. Your children need to learn how to manage time, care for their property, and spend their money wisely. Your children also need to know how to control their thoughts, tongue and temper. On and on it goes, endlessly.

Children come into the world with thousands upon thousands of needs. And the greatest need of them all is this: *they need a wise, loving and Godly father who will be their pastor!*

Will you be that man?

A Personal Application

What practical advice does Solomon have for fathers in Proverbs 4:1-9? How can you apply this passage?

_____
_____
_____
_____
_____
_____
_____
_____
_____
_____
_____
_____
_____
_____
_____
_____
_____
_____
_____
_____

WEEK TEN - Day 2

Pastoring Your Children (2)

There is much more to pastoring your children than making them happy; you must also make them holy!

The apostle Paul describes the work of a good pastor in Acts 20. Here he identifies his main responsibilities.

First, the good pastor (and good father) is to guard his own soul from dangers — like self-centeredness, anger, misplaced priorities, lust, prayerlessness, foul language, and the like. As a FATHER FOR GOD your first duty is to beware of everything that can hinder your own walk with God. Wherever there is temptation, you must detect it, detest it, and soundly defeat it! Everything depends on your character!

Second, the good pastor (and good father) is to do everything possible to lead his children to Jesus Christ and salvation. This means from infancy onward every Godly father will explain to his children the message of sin, guilt, divine justice, grace and forgiveness.

Third, the good pastor (and good father) is to protect his children from false teachings at school, on television, on the internet, and from friends. You are to help your children both believe and behave spiritually.

How are you doing?

A Personal Application

Read Acts 20:22-30. Based on these verses, how passionate do you need to be in order to become a true father for God? Where do you need to make improvements?

_____
_____
_____
_____
_____
_____
_____
_____
_____
_____
_____
_____
_____
_____
_____
_____
_____
_____
_____
_____

WEEK TEN - Day 3

Pastoring Your Children (3)

The best fathers on earth lead by example.

According to the apostle Paul, a good pastor will be a man who is strong with three virtues: *(1) Christ-centeredness, (2) character, and (3) competence.* In the same way, every FATHER FOR GOD will be respected by his wife and children for possessing these qualities. Take a moment and memorize these three traits.

A good pastor (and a good father) will also watch his flock affectionately both day and night. Every little detail of their lives is always his utmost concern.

Another duty of a good pastor (and father) is teaching the Bible. The spiritual FATHER FOR GOD will make it a key priority to read the Bible (along with other Christian literature) *daily* to his younger children. And he will train his older children to have their own time for *daily* devotions. This is critical in the formation of children and youth!

Finally, a good pastor (and father) will pray every day for his sheep. Godly fathers must pray both *for* and *with* their children about everything: school, friends, hurt feelings, desires, struggles, and so on.

How large and active of a role do you play in the lives of your children? Should you do more?

A Personal Application

Finish reading Paul's testimony in Acts 20:31-38. What attitude do you find here that should be in every father's heart?

_____
_____
_____
_____
_____
_____
_____
_____
_____
_____
_____
_____
_____
_____
_____
_____
_____
_____
_____
_____

WEEK TEN - Day 4

Conquering Their Will (1)

Children need more than direction; they also need discipline.

Children are not the sweet little angels that fairy-tale books would like you to believe. While they are basically *good*, because they are made in God's image, they are even more basically *bad* because they are born with a sinful disposition as well. For instance, if children don't get *what* they want *when* they want it, they will eventually prove their innate corruption to you! Therefore, one of your first duties as a responsible FATHER FOR GOD is to conquer your child's will.

This concept sounds almost extreme in today's all-tolerant culture, but it has actually been a fundamental rule in parenting for centuries prior to our modern period. If you fail here, your children will likely end up spoiled and annoyingly self-centered. But if you conquer their will early on (between birth and age two), then they will learn to live for their parent's wishes, instead of their own. When that happens, parents will maintain their headship of the home, children will follow directions without arguing, and an atmosphere of peace will prevail!

Really, how well have you mastered the will of your children? Do they respect your ideas and rules?

A Personal Application

Closely examine the following Proverbs. Explain the attitude God wants to see developed in Godly children. Look at 10:1; 15:5, 20; 17:21, 25; and 23:15-16.

_____
_____
_____
_____
_____
_____
_____
_____
_____
_____
_____
_____
_____
_____
_____
_____
_____
_____
_____
_____
_____

WEEK TEN - Day 5

Conquering Their Will (2)

Until children say to their parents, "Not my will, but yours be done," their sinful nature needs to be conquered.

The following analogy seems crude, but it makes an important point: *some kids are like undisciplined dogs* — they don't come when they are called, they don't sit still when you tell them not to move, they don't stop talking when you tell them to be quiet . . . and so on!

More than a few kindergarten and first grade teachers will tell you that many of the kids who come to them are not ready for school because their parents have not trained them to follow simple directions or to respect authority. They are a lot like neighborhood dogs on the loose. Of course, no parent will admit their children are like that, but teachers (including Sunday School teachers) will disagree.

One of the most critical duties of every FATHER FOR GOD is to train his children over and over and over, until they want — from the heart — to honor and obey their parents, teachers and other authority figures in their life. No child is ready for school (or heaven!) until they pass this test.

Are all of your children prompt to obey with a positive and respectful attitude?

A Personal Application

How successful have you become in reproducing the following Proverbs in your home? See 19:13a; 23:22-25 and 29:3a.

_____
_____
_____
_____
_____
_____
_____
_____
_____
_____
_____
_____
_____
_____
_____
_____
_____
_____

WEEK TEN - Days 6-7

Thinking It Through

Take two days to review the previous five lessons. Write out a prayer that reflects what you desire to apply from these lessons.

WEEK ELEVEN - Day 1

Setting the Example

Children may do what you TELL them, but they are more likely to do what you SHOW them.

If you want your children to be good, then there is a basic rule you must follow: *you must first be good yourself.* Children can see hypocrisy a mile away, and they hate it as much as you do. Therefore, if you want your children to do the right thing, day after day, then you must set a consistent example for them by also doing the right thing.

The FATHER FOR GOD does more than correct his children when they display a negative attitude, speak an offensive word or show disrespect. They correct themselves, too. When their own attitude, words or actions are wrong, they admit it and apologize — they apologize to their wives and to their children!

FATHERS FOR GOD will not hold their children to a higher standard than they themselves are willing to follow. Instead, they will insist that *everyone* in the family live by the same rules: *God's rules in the Bible*.

What about you? Are you a good example for your wife and children? Do the members of your own family look up to you with respect?

A Personal Application

Read Matthew 7:21-27, and identify at least two critical points that you can apply in your own life and home.

WEEK ELEVEN - Day 2

Insisting on Obedience

God looks for the same thing in both parents and children: OBEDIENCE.

Joy Dawson, a popular teacher for Youth With A Mission, has wisely identified three ingredients in genuine obedience. Is this the kind of obedience you require from your own children?

- First, in true obedience there is *promptness*. This means you must do what you're told to do when you're told to do it. Procrastination is simply disobedience.

- Second, in the kind of obedience that God accepts there is *thoroughness*. A job that is only half-done is not done at all.

- Third, in pure obedience there is *a positive attitude*. Grumpy "obedience" is unacceptable. We must obey with a cheerful heart.

Most parents tell their children over and over to do the same thing. This is bad parenting. You must mean what you say, and you must train your children to believe you the first time you tell them something.

Do your children obey you promptly, thoroughly and with a positive attitude?

A Personal Application

Just as God sees that there are consequences for sin, so fathers should see that there are consequences for disobedience in the home. How is this fact explained in Proverbs 13:24; 19:18; 22:15; 23:13-14; 29:15 and 17?

_____
_____
_____
_____
_____
_____
_____
_____
_____
_____
_____
_____
_____
_____
_____
_____
_____
_____
_____
_____

WEEK ELEVEN - Day 3

Insisting on Obedience (2)

Fathers who teach their children full obedience prepare them to walk humbly with God!

FATHERS FOR GOD are more than men who raise children; they are also God's *representatives*. In other words, every father is responsible to reflect the same kind of parenting practices that God our Heavenly Father employs! Let me explain.

First, this means that parents are to *reward* their children when they comply with family laws and God's laws. There should be lots of hugs, kisses, laughter and happiness in a Godly home. Children and youth in this home should know that it pays well to live in obedience.

Second, this means that parents are to *punish* sons and daughters when they defy family laws and God's laws. There should be a clear understanding by everyone of the specific consequences that will take place for breaking the rules, and there should be no delay in dispensing the discipline when that line has been crossed.

Children who learn at home how to obey their parents from the heart will know how to obey God the same way!

A Personal Application

What does the Lord have to say about discipline in Hebrews 12:1-11 that you need to apply in your home?

_____
_____
_____
_____
_____
_____
_____
_____
_____
_____
_____
_____
_____
_____
_____
_____
_____
_____
_____
_____
_____

WEEK ELEVEN - Day 4

Insisting on Obedience (3)

Obedience and disobedience do not go unnoticed by God, and they must not go unnoticed by fathers either.

When God looks at your life, He either *blesses* or *curses* you because of what He finds in four areas: (1) the desires of your heart, (2) the thoughts of your mind, (3) the words of your mouth, and (4) the decisions of your will.

When the Lord finds obedience in your desires, thoughts, speech and decisions, He blesses you. When He finds a pattern of disobedience in any of these areas, He curses you. In the same way, you need to be prepared to reward and punish your children for their behavior in these same four areas.

Sometimes you can discipline a child for inappropriate speech and actions, but you must always go deeper than that. FATHERS FOR GOD are concerned about motives and attitudes as well. Correction must involve more than a response to the obvious external things you see. You must also confront and correct the internal things that are sometimes less obvious.

When your children behave like weeds, do more than stop the misbehavior. Dig down into their thoughts and desires. Remove the roots that created the weeds in the first place.

A Personal Application

Read Deuteronomy 28:1-19, then identify at least three ways you can apply this passage in your home.

WEEK ELEVEN - Day 5

Living in God's Presence

If you will learn to practice the presence of God in your home, you will bring glory to the Lord and blessings to yourself!

The purpose for living is the same for everyone, whether you be a child, youth or adult. We are all made to glorify God in every area of our life. This is our full-time occupation. When we are at home, our motive should be to bring God glory. When we are at work, school, or elsewhere, our motive must always be to glorify God.

The Christian's life is *not* divided into two categories: (1) sacred and (2) secular. Instead, for the followers of Jesus Christ, everything we do, we perform it as if God were present watching us. Therefore, we try to please Him every day, in every place, and under every circumstance.

This means it is the foremost duty of parents (especially fathers), to train their children in this way of thinking. FATHERS FOR GOD are to equip their sons and daughters with a heart that never forgets they are always in the presence of God — He sees, He hears, and He is prepared to help.

In order for your children and youth to develop this spiritual habit, you will need to remind them often of God's power, promises and presence. Do you do that?

A Personal Application

How can you teach your children the message of Romans 8:5-17? Give specific ideas.

_____
_____
_____
_____
_____
_____
_____
_____
_____
_____
_____
_____
_____
_____
_____
_____
_____

WEEK ELEVEN - Days 6-7

Thinking It Through

Take two days to review the previous five lessons. Write out a prayer that reflects what you desire to apply from these lessons.

WEEK TWELVE - Day 1

Dating Your Children

Children and youth do not believe you love them because you say you do, but because you prove it in personal ways.

Children and youth need to know deeply that they are special to God and special to their father. One of the best ways you can do this is by setting aside one day a month (as a minimum) to take them out on a date.

The normal routine at home between fathers and their children should be positive, transparent and meaningful, but there is no substitute for special occasions when Dads go the extra mile to bless their kids. There are a million things you can do on a date, but the two most important things are these: (1) Go where your child would like to go — honor his (or her) reasonable desires. And (2), talk a lot — about family life, school matters, personal issues, and God's heart.

The goal behind dating your children is to demonstrate both your love and God's love for them. It is a time for extra encouragement, counseling, attentive listening, and bonding. It is a time for good old-fashioned fun. Eat together. Shop together. Play together. And most of all, just talk — heart to heart.

A Personal Application

Successful parenting depends a great deal on how well you love your kids. Identify three or four things you can take from 1 Corinthians 13 to improve your own love.

_____
_____
_____
_____
_____
_____
_____
_____
_____
_____
_____
_____
_____
_____
_____
_____
_____
_____

WEEK TWELVE - Day 2

Going to Bed Properly

Pillows and prayers are a perfect match.

When children are left to themselves, they will live undisciplined lives. And one of the areas where they will be least disciplined is the manner in which they choose to go to bed. Therefore, one of the early duties you have as a FATHER FOR GOD is to see to it that your children know *when* and *how* to go to bed. There is more to this ritual than putting on pajamas and crawling under a sheet. There are two other matters that need to take place as well.

First, children (and adults!) need to go to bed with all of their conflicts either resolved or confidently left in God's care. No one should try going to sleep with relationships or circumstances upside down. FATHERS FOR GOD must help their children retire every night at peace!

Second, children (and adults!) need to go to bed with prayers — their own prayers and your prayers for them. It should be a fixed routine for Dad or Mom to tuck the children in bed with a prayer. Of course, children should also be taught to go to be early enough that this time with God and parents is not rushed or mechanical.

Is the Lord in the center of how you tell your children good night?

A Personal Application

Psalm 16 is a good night-time passage. How can you use these verses to help your children go to sleep?

_____
_____
_____
_____
_____
_____
_____
_____
_____
_____
_____
_____
_____
_____
_____
_____
_____
_____
_____

WEEK TWELVE - Day 3

Getting Up Properly

Never get up to face the world; get up to greet the Word!

Secular families often get up late, listen to the radio or television, eat a quick bite, then rush off to school or work. Many Christian families follow this same godless pattern. Don't let this be the habit in *your* home!

If you will go to bed reasonably early, then you will be able to get up reasonably early — early enough to spend some quality time with the Lord before you do anything else. FATHERS FOR GOD need to train themselves and their children until they understand that if Jesus is truly first in their *life*, then he will also be first in their *day!*

This means that parents should read the Bible thoughtfully and/or pray patiently ever morning. It also means they should get their children up in time to deposit some Scripture and prayer in their minds before they go to school. Children and youth need to begin their day with God, with the Bible, and with prayer. You need to be your children's example in this practice.

Pray for a moment, and answer this question: *What kind of routine does the Lord want you to follow each morning in your home?*

A Personal Application

Great men have great mornings — great mornings with God. Read the following passages, then write out the way you can have great mornings. See Psalm 5:3; 92:1-4; Lamentations 3:22-23 and Mark 1:35

_____
_____
_____
_____
_____
_____
_____
_____
_____
_____
_____
_____
_____
_____
_____
_____
_____

WEEK TWELVE - Day 4

Making "Free" Time Productive (1)

Your home should be the center of productive and fun living.

Each week the average teenager spends a whopping fifty-six hours on cell phones, watching television and movies, exploring the internet, and playing video games! That's a total of eight hours per day (or the equivalent of a full-time job with sixteen hours of overtime)! On the other hand, the typical Dad spends only seven to eight minutes per day one-on-one with his children! Do you see the problem?

It is impossible for a father to raise his children to love God's values if he permits a million and one other things to influence them the vast majority of the time. From the earliest periods in a child's life he or she needs to learn that the family and productive projects come first, second and third (*before* friends, entertainment, sports, band practice, the computer, TV, and so on).

Until children discover the greater joy of being a fulfilled family and working on useful projects together, they will attempt to find their primary happiness in either superficial activities or in things outside of the home. Really, how wisely do you and your children use your "free" time?

A Personal Application

Read Ecclesiastes 2:24-26; 3:9-13 and 12:13-14. What does your family do during its "free" time?

WEEK TWELVE - Day 5

Making "Free" Time Productive (2)

When family members love each other more than anything else, there is no better place than home.

Healthy families deeply enjoy being at home and doing things together. Therefore, every FATHER FOR GOD must find ways to make home life profoundly interesting, productive and fun.

Instead of investing yourself in activities of minimal lasting value, here's a short list of things your family should consider doing together: read books out loud, watch teaching videos (especially on Christian teachings, history and biographies), grow a garden, remodel a room (or the basement or the whole house), develop a high level of skill in some hobby (like photography, playing an instrument, scrap booking, sewing, cooking, woodworking, drawing, and so on). Set aside one day a month to help a needy person with housework or lawn care or something else. Go to the library and conduct interesting research. Join the 4-H Club and present a project at the county Fair. Go on field trips. Play games together. Take on a spiritual ministry project that utilizes everyone in the family (like a missions trip or a visit to a nursing home, and the like). There are tens of thousands of productive things you and your family can do.

Dads, make your home great!

A Personal Application

Carefully read Proverbs 3. Then, think of a half-dozen ways you and your kids could spend your "free" time more productively.

WEEK TWELVE - Days 6-7

Thinking It Through

Take two days to review the previous five lessons. Write out a prayer that reflects what you desire to apply from these lessons.

WEEK THIRTEEN - Day 1

A Bible-Centered Home

The surest way for families to become worldly is to neglect family devotions.

As much as we hate to admit it, the truth is that many "Christian" homes are worldly. When fathers do not set aside time for personal prayer and Bible reading, there is a measure of worldliness in the family. When mothers do not have significant daily devotions, there is more worldliness in the home. And when parents do not oversee some sort of daily devotions for their children, there is even more worldliness in the household. There simply is no other way to say it: *Homes that are not Bible-centered are world-centered!*

When the Pilgrims came to America, they brought with them their Bible, along with some unique practices. It was the habit of the Pilgrim parents to rise between four and five o'clock for lengthy devotions. Afterward, the whole family would eat breakfast together. Then, the father would lead his family in prayer and Bible study for one full hour! Next, came school and work. At the end of the day the father would again lead his family in another hour of prayer and Bible study! This pattern took place every day!

You may not follow this pattern, but as a FATHER FOR GOD it is your duty (and privilege) to lead your family "by the Book." How are you doing?

A Personal Application

Read Deuteronomy 6:1-9 and Ephesians 6:1-4. Pray and ask the Lord how He would like you to lead your family "by the Book."

_____
_____
_____
_____
_____
_____
_____
_____
_____
_____
_____
_____
_____
_____
_____
_____
_____
_____
_____
_____

WEEK THIRTEEN - Day 2

Ending the Chaos

When a family is on the go from dawn to dusk, it usually isn't going anywhere that matters.

Every FATHER FOR GOD must take a long, hard look at his family's weekly routine and answer this question: *Is our family Christ-centered, or is it work-centered, or parent-centered, or child-centered?*

In more than a few homes the schedule is overly crowded with work, school, after-school activities, trips to this and that, appointments, weekend plans, television routines, time spent with friends (either in person or on the phone or on the internet), and so on. The average home is busy, busy, busy. And on the surface, everyone seems to think this is normal. But eventually wise families discover that busyness can actually rob their home of the togetherness they need . . . they learn the hard way that the more they stuff into their schedules, the less they add to their family's wholeness.

The bottom line is this: *many families need more time for themselves.* Too many activities (especially child-centered "fun" activities) can decentralize the home and turn it into a stressful whirlwind.

Honestly, do you pray before you make commitments for yourself and for the members of your family?

A Personal Application

Read Psalm 127, and answer this question: "Is Jesus in charge of your calendar and commitments?"

WEEK THIRTEEN - Day 3

Picking the Right School (1)

If you won't permit your children to watch certain TV shows, why would you permit them to attend schools where the values of these immoral shows are encouraged?

It should be the most obvious fact on earth, but sadly it is not only often unrecognized, it is even frequently dismissed: *If you want your children to become strong in the Lord and develop a mature Christian worldview, then you must seriously consider either a Christian school or homeschool for them.*

Today's public schools are not the same institutions they were twenty years ago. Just think for a moment. At what cost do you send your child to a school where prayer and Bible reading are forbidden? Do you really want to send your children to schools that literally welcome the homosexual lifestyle, premarital sex and abortions?

Honestly, can you expose your children to a secular-oriented education seven hours a day, five days a week, for twelve years and then expect spiritual results? Don't kid yourself into believing that the average public school is okay. Consider this shocking fact: *Over 90% of all church youth who attend public schools do not continue attending church after high school!* Of course there are exceptions, but 90% is simply too many youth! You can do better than that!

A Personal Application

Read 2 Timothy 3:14-17 two times. How thoughtful have you been in picking the right school for your children? Why is this so important?

_____
_____
_____
_____
_____
_____
_____
_____
_____
_____
_____
_____
_____
_____
_____
_____
_____
_____
_____

WEEK THIRTEEN - Day 4

Picking the Right School (2)

If your son or daughter wanted to become a great portrait photographer, would you send them to a Playboy studio to learn their skill?

You can't raise spiritual children in a worldly environment any more than you can raise good vegetables in the dark! Plants require lots of light; so do your children.

It isn't cheap to send children to a quality Christian school or to homeschool them. It takes money. It takes time. But aren't your children worth it? And isn't your God big enough to help with the time and finances so you can raise your children to become spiritual champions?

Every FATHER OF GOD must set aside the necessary funds to see that his children get a *Christian* education. More than that, every grandparent should do the same thing for their grandchildren. And even more than that, every church should provide partial or whole scholarships for each of its member's children. There is no better way to spend money than on the spiritual education of children and youth!

Naturally, there will be kids who go to Christian schools or who are homeschooled who don't turn out well, but isn't it much more likely that the majority of the kids will turn out alright? Of course. Let's do it!

A Personal Application

Read Colossians 2:6-10 twice. What can you and your church do to educate children in Christian truth?

_____
_____
_____
_____
_____
_____
_____
_____
_____
_____
_____
_____
_____
_____
_____
_____
_____
_____
_____
_____
_____
_____

WEEK THIRTEEN - Day 5

Making Good Christians

Today's Christian children should be prepared to become tomorrow's finest representatives for God.

Before your children are conceived or born in this world, you should possess one driving ambition for their lives: *that they would live moment by moment for the glory of God and for the eternal good of people!*

The world does not need more *people*, and the church does not need more *members*. What the world and the church need are more good Christians — men and women who are endowed with a Christ-centered worldview, an impeccable character, and a top notch competence. This is what we need. And this is what good family (normally) produce.

FATHERS FOR GOD see more than what their children are at any given moment. They see what their children can become; and they envision the kind of difference their children can make in this world. Therefore, they prepare their children for the rigors of this world and for the rewards of the world to come. They train them to live in the light of eternity!

Dad, is this your passion?

A Personal Application

Are you raising your children in the light of the Great Commission and the Great Commandments? Explain. See Matthew 28:19-20 and Mark 12:28-31.

WEEK THIRTEEN - Days 6-7

Thinking It Through

Take two days to review the previous five lessons. Write out a prayer that reflects what you desire to apply from these lessons.

What it Means to be
A CHURCHMAN FOR GOD

WEEK FOURTEEN - Day 1

Embrace Your Five Callings

A man is not complete until he finds and fulfills the five callings God has placed on his life.

If you were to ask the average man on the street to identify his five callings from God, he'd probably have a difficult time listing them. Unfortunately, more than a few men *in the church* face the same predicament. They need focus. They need to know their five purposes in life.

From infancy, boys should be taught that God has five callings (or five major plans) for their lives. They should be taught and trained to be . . .

- MEN of God
- HUSBANDS for God
- FATHERS for God
- CHURCHMEN for God
- WITNESSES for God

The foremost work of every church should be to knead these truths into male children, youth and adults (naturally, girls need to understand their five callings as well). It is here — in the local church — where men are to learn how to be true men!

Does your church have highly competent and comprehensive programs for preparing its men to fulfill their five callings?

A Personal Application

In order to reach the proper destination you must have the proper starting point. How does Paul describe the right starting point in Romans 12:1-2? How can you live out these two verses?

_____
_____
_____
_____
_____
_____
_____
_____
_____
_____
_____
_____
_____
_____
_____
_____
_____
_____
_____
_____

WEEK FOURTEEN - Day 2

Every Man's Five Callings

The greatest need in the world is for men like you to excel in fulfilling God's five callings.

1. MEN OF GOD are the Lord's key disciples. They do not live to fulfill their own agendas, but to find and follow God's agenda day after day.

2. HUSBANDS FOR GOD are their wive's first pastor. They conscientiously oversee the salvation and spiritual formation of their spouses.

3. PARENTS FOR GOD are their children's first and primary pastor. They take seriously the conversion and spiritual development of their children.

4. CHURCHMEN FOR GOD are the Lord's key ministers. They are men who receive intense teaching and training so they can be equipped to serve the Lord's Church and make a difference in peoples' lives.

5. WITNESSES FOR GOD are the Lord's ambassadors to the world. With passion and skill they are able to lead people to Jesus Christ and salvation.

How are you doing in your callings?

A Personal Application

There are four possible heart-responses you can have to God's callings? You can be (1) hard, (2) shallow, (3) distracted, or (4) fully receptive. Read Luke 8:1-15, and explain which "soil" (or heart) best identifies you.

WEEK FOURTEEN - Day 3

Why Go to Church?

The church exists to help men fulfill their five God-given callings.

Approximately 43% of the adults in church are men, but the more critical issue is this: *How many of these men are actually CHURCHMEN FOR GOD?* Probably very few. Here's why.

- Often churches do not offer men a high enough level of *teaching and training* to prepare them for significant spiritual ministry at home, in the church, or in the community. Men need to be challenged, stretched and motivated to a higher level.

- Often men follow the path of least responsibility, which stunts their growth and paralyzes their usefulness. They are lazy when it comes to spiritual disciplines.

If you are going to become a true CHURCHMAN FOR GOD, then both of the above problems must be overcome. First, you must prepare your own heart for meaningful spiritual growth and service. Second, your church must prepare high-level opportunities that will literally make a difference in your life.

Are you and your church ready?

A Personal Application

Based on 1 Peter 4:10-11, what has the Lord done to help you become a churchman for God? How has He gifted you personally?

_____
_____
_____
_____
_____
_____
_____
_____
_____
_____
_____
_____
_____
_____
_____
_____
_____
_____
_____
_____

WEEK FOURTEEN - Day 4

Ministry Verses Meetings

In a healthy church the people on the platform train the people in the pews to become effective ministers!

The true measure of a successful church can be found in just one key area: *how many people does it develop into fruitful workers for the Lord?* Anything less than this ambition is pretend Christianity!

Only churches that find ways to turn spiritual wimps into true MEN of God, HUSBANDS for God, FATHERS for God, CHURCHMEN for God, and WITNESSES for God are considered successful by the Lord. Shallow men may enjoy counting nickels (the size of the offerings) and noses (the size of the attendance), but God uses another measuring stick. He looks at the "ministry factor."

In the mind of God there are only three types of CHURCHMEN FOR GOD: (1) those who are trainers, (2) those who are trainees, (3) and those who are engaged in some sort of spiritual ministry. He doesn't care how many *meetings* are conducted; His focus is always on how many *ministries* are literally transforming lives and helping people. He expects the church to change men, to equip men, and to use men to make a difference!

A Personal Application

Read Ephesians 4:11-13, then explain the work God has planned for both church leaders and men. Is this happening in yourself and in your church?

_____
_____
_____
_____
_____
_____
_____
_____
_____
_____
_____
_____
_____
_____
_____
_____
_____
_____
_____
_____

WEEK FOURTEEN - Day 5

Developing Men

*If you target women,
you will reach women and children.
If you target men,
you will reach whole families.*

Every church should be designed from the ground up to reach and use men to the maximum. Women are a vital part of the church, too, but impacting men must become every church's top priority. Here's why:

- When a church targets women, they will be able to bring their whole family to church just 17% of the time.

- When a church targets men, they will be able to bring their whole family to church a colossal 93% of the time!

- In more than 80% of all churches in the United States there is a woman's ministry, but a man's ministry can be found in less than 10% of all churches. This is critical because 90% of all young men will leave church in their twenties, thinking church is for children and women, not them.

What is your church doing to impact *men* for God? How effectively does your church train men for ministry?

A Personal Application

Read God's calling of Jeremiah in Jeremiah 1:4-10, 17-19. Can you envision God calling you to some work? Explain.

_____
_____
_____
_____
_____
_____
_____
_____
_____
_____
_____
_____
_____
_____
_____
_____
_____
_____
_____
_____

WEEK FOURTEEN - Days 6-7

Thinking It Through

Take two days to review the previous five lessons. Write out a prayer that reflects what you desire to apply from these lessons.

WEEK FIFTEEN - Day 1

Spiritual Power for Men

Churchmen for God enjoy church music and messages, but most of all they hunger to be involved and make a difference!

When a man becomes a Christian, the Holy Spirit deposits a spiritual gift in his soul so he can use it to help others. There are more than twenty unique gifts mentioned in the New Testament. Some are *leadership abilities,* others are *speaking skills,* and still others are special enablements to *help people* in practical ways (of course, people with speaking gifts will serve, and individuals with serving gifts may speak; there is an overlap in all of the gifts). These unique spiritual gifts are found in Romans 12:3-7; 1 Corinthians 12:4-11, 28; and Ephesians 4:11.

Only the Holy Spirit can build a CHURCHMAN, and He does so by giving him three things: (1) a heart for God, (2) a hatred for sin, and (3) a hunger to bless people through His gifts! Whatever else you do, be sure you pray diligently for these three anointings!

The church needs men — more men — who will step out of the pew and resolve to make a difference. Will you do everything you can to find your niche and help? You — *yes, you!* — can be used in important ways by God. Believe it! Act on it!

A Personal Application

Itemize the gifts you find in these passages: Romans 12:3-7; 1 Corinthians 12:4-11, 28; and Ephesians 4:11. Can you see yourself employing one or several of these gifts? Explain your answer.

WEEK FIFTEEN - Day 2

Leadership Development (1)

Mature men must lead other men into maturity.

In every business, new employees are trained by a skillful leader until they can perform a service by themselves. This may take a day, a week, a month or longer. But in the end, the new employee eventually provides a valuable service for the business.

In the average church, new male members are often trained to do four things: (1) sit, (2) sing, (3) give in the offering, and (4) return the following week to repeat this same superficial ritual. In the end, new male members rarely provide valuable ministry for their church beyond that of greeting people and ushering. We can do better than that!

The church must conduct meetings *by* men, *for* men, and *about practical spiritual issues that pertain to men.* In addition to this, staff members and other mature leaders must be responsible to handpick and train at least two or three men *per year* until their characters are solid, their homes are operating properly, and their confidence to serve the Lord is strong.

Men must discover that they matter to God, and that they can make a difference helping people at home, at church, and in the world!

A Personal Application

Read Mark 3:13-19, and identify at least two ways a church could carry out the essence of this passage today . . . with you.

_____
_____
_____
_____
_____
_____
_____
_____
_____
_____
_____
_____
_____
_____
_____
_____
_____
_____
_____
_____
_____

WEEK FIFTEEN - Day 3

Leadership Development (2)

When our standards are low, we make men like the world; when our standards are high, we make men like God!

Nowhere in the Bible is the church charged with the duty to make "members." Instead, it is commanded to make "disciples." A true "disciple" is an apprentice — a person who undergoes comprehensive training in order to acquire knowledge and skill.

In the modern world, for example, an electrical apprentice will go to school two nights per week for five years, read textbooks and take tests pertaining to his occupation. Additionally, he will work for 10,000 hours under a professional electrician before he is qualified to lead others — *that* is an apprentice (or disciple). Sadly, we require more academic expertise and more hands-on experience from electricians than we do for most Christian ministers!

If the local church is going to make true "disciples," then it must add some "meat" to its educational and experiential ministries. We have relied on marshmallows (things soft and sweet) too long! It's time we dig much deeper. It's time we raise the standards. It's time we provide academics and ministry opportunities that will make us stretch!

A Personal Application

Read Matthew 10, and identify at least two ways a church could carry out the essence of this passage today . . . with you.

_____
_____
_____
_____
_____
_____
_____
_____
_____
_____
_____
_____
_____
_____
_____
_____
_____
_____
_____
_____
_____
_____

WEEK FIFTEEN - Day 4

Leadership Development (3)

Jesus didn't make disciples between ten o'clock and noon on Sundays. What makes us think we can?

Imagine your son going to school for the first time. He proudly gets on the bus Monday morning and goes to the local elementary school. Once there, everyone files into a large auditorium where the assistant principal leads everyone in a couple of songs. Then the principal stands up and speaks for a while. When this is over, everyone gets back on the bus to return home. One week later this same routine is repeated . . . week after week, month after month, for twelve years!

Question: At the end of this twelve-year period, how many students will be able to read their diploma?

This illustration closely parallels how the average church conducts its work. They have members come once a week for an hour or two, then send them home for a week. This practice is often repeated for a whole lifetime!

Question: At the end of a dozen years or so, how many of these church members will be mature? Is this routine acceptable to you? If not, what can be done?

A Personal Application

Read Acts 2:37-47, and identify at least two ways a church could carry out the essence of this passage today . . . with you.

WEEK FIFTEEN - Day 5

Leadership Development (4)

Men of the church will not make a difference until they detest personal and church wide lukewarmness.

Out of all the things the devil does, he works the hardest to achieve these two objectives: keep lost people lost, and keep saved people ineffective (especially Christian men). Unfortunately, the devil has been remarkably successful. But that *can* change. Satan *can* be defeated. And men *can* lead the way!

This will happen when men finally rise up and say with one voice: "We have attended enough meetings, we have heard enough sermons, and we have sung enough songs. We want to start making a real difference — *an everlasting difference* — in people's lives! We want to do something that matters! We want to be trained for life-changing ministry!"

Content people will change nothing; they will not rock the boat. But frustrated people who have a passion to see every man living in God's five callings will not rest until every man he knows is changed!

Honestly, will you ask the Lord to change you? Then, will you ask the Lord to use you and your church to help other men change?

A Personal Application

Read Judges 6, then look around at the Christian men you know. How many of them could become like Gideon? Could you become like Gideon? Explain.

_____
_____
_____
_____
_____
_____
_____
_____
_____
_____
_____
_____
_____
_____
_____
_____
_____
_____
_____

WEEK FIFTEEN - Days 6-7

Thinking It Through

Take two days to review the previous five lessons. Write out a prayer that reflects what you desire to apply from these lessons.

WEEK SIXTEEN - Day 1

Ministry that Matters (1)

Dying churches have one meeting after another, while dynamic churches have one ministry after another.

No man will find his ultimate purpose for life in a book, in a seminar, or in a church. All of these things are fine and necessary, but a CHURCHMAN FOR GOD finds his purpose and fulfillment in the midst of actual *ministry*.

Attending church meetings isn't enough. Singing songs isn't enough. Giving cash in the offerings isn't enough. Ushering and greeting people isn't enough. CHURCHMEN FOR GOD want more; they need more. They know that the real work of God is not limited merely to attending their church faithfully. They may sit in the pew, but they want God's power, too. They want to help people in significant ways; they want to engage in ministry that matters! And they don't care if that ministry takes place inside or outside the church building, as long as lives are being transformed on a regular basis.

CHURCHMEN FOR GOD want to make a difference — a real difference. So they seek out opportunities to meet needs; they get involved. They refuse to live on the sidelines. Does this sound like you? Are you proactive when it comes to ministry?

A Personal Application

Read Matthew 25:14-30. What kinds of practical and eternal investments are you making with the resources God has given to you?

_____
_____
_____
_____
_____
_____
_____
_____
_____
_____
_____
_____
_____
_____
_____
_____
_____
_____
_____

WEEK SIXTEEN - Day 2

Ministry that Matters (2)

There will be no real maturity in a Churchman for God until he is regularly engaged in a meaningful ministry.

The CHURCHMAN FOR GOD looks at his fellow men and says, "Lord, use us *more!* Make us *ministers!* Make us *effective!*" He knows that the key to every man's growth and success depends in large part on his involvement in ministries that impact lives.

For some men, significant ministry will mean one-on-one mentoring of a young man or two every Saturday morning at a restaurant. For others, it will mean some kind of regular spiritual service to the inmates at a local prison. For still others, they will find their purpose and fulfillment in ministries like these: teaching a Sunday School class, helping the elderly with home or car repairs, making routine visits in the hospital or nursing homes, assisting families develop a budget in order to get out of debt, working with parents of difficult children, overseeing a food bank, visiting the visitors who come to your church, engaging in evangelism projects, helping other men find and follow the five callings God has for them, and so on.

There simply is no limit to the number of things God may place on your heart to impact people's lives. You should pray every day for ministry opportunities. Begin where you live and work!

A Personal Application

Identify at least three practical ministry principles you can find in these verses: 1 Corinthians 15:58 and Galatians 6:7-10. Passionately pray through your list.

WEEK SIXTEEN - Day 3

Ministry that Matters (3)

Ministries that last are built on a foundation of compelling passion and careful plans.

Effective ministry doesn't *just* happen. It requires prayer, insight and perseverance. Here are four basic tips for the CHURCHMAN FOR GOD who wants to get more out of his Christian life.

1. Pray to be used by God. Find out what He would like you to do to help people. Get specific. Persevere.

2. Look for other effective ministries who are already doing what you want to do. Consider joining them. If you can't find any such ministry, recruit like-minded people to work with you. Develop your own special team of ministers.

3. Develop a ministry schedule. Don't fall into the trap of doing things "when you can get around to it." Open your calendar and set a fixed time for prayer, for skill development, and for actual ministry.

4. Record and report your ministry results to your church's leadership. Accountability and fresh testimonies are foundational to success.

A Personal Application

After reading Matthew 25:31-46, identify at least two major reasons why you should be engaged in some kind of regular ministry.

_____
_____
_____
_____
_____
_____
_____
_____
_____
_____
_____
_____
_____
_____
_____
_____
_____
_____

WEEK SIXTEEN - Day 4

Ministry that Matters (4)

The first step in effective ministry is to make an honest evaluation.

Church leaders and interested CHURCHMEN FOR GOD need to work in harmony until they have peace about the answers to the following questions:

1. Is our church focused primarily on getting people to attend *meetings*, or is the emphasis on getting men involved in *ministries that make a difference in people's lives?*

2. Do we have an effective strategy for recruiting, training and releasing men (and women) for ministry?

3. What are the current in-house and out-of-house ministries that are actually transforming lives? Are these ministries sufficiently staffed and adequately financed?

4. Do we have ineffective ministries that need new leaders? Do we have ineffective ministries that need to be discontinued? Are there new ministries the Lord would like us to add to our list?

5. Am I personally involved in a ministry that matches my abilities and passion? Am I effective?

A Personal Application

Think of at least two ways your church can get every member to fulfill James 2:14-20.

WEEK SIXTEEN - Day 5

Ministry that Matters (5)

No single church is large enough or talented enough to impact everyone God wants to transform.

For the average male church member, loyalty resides almost exclusively within the four walls of his own congregation and denomination. But for the CHURCHMAN OF GOD this is only a starting point.

The CHURCHMAN OF GOD sees beyond traditional boundaries. He can see other spiritual churches that want to accomplish the same objectives he wants. He can see his whole community. He can envision the larger Kingdom of God, and not just his own little slice of the pie. Therefore, he is not opposed to helping any Christian or any church in any way because he views them as equal comrades, not competitors or enemies. More than that, he sees other spiritual churches as resources that can help him and his own congregation.

The more a church is *independent*, the more it isolates itself from significant community ministry. However, the more a church is *interdependent*, the more it can impact the values and decisions of a whole region! Are you and your church open to cooperating with the whole body of Christ?

A Personal Application

Read 1 John 4:7-21, and explain with specific examples the heart of genuine ministry.

_____
_____
_____
_____
_____
_____
_____
_____
_____
_____
_____
_____
_____
_____
_____
_____
_____
_____
_____
_____
_____

WEEK SIXTEEN - Days 6-7

Thinking It Through

Take two days to review the previous five lessons. Write out a prayer that reflects what you desire to apply from these lessons.

WEEK SEVENTEEN - Day 1

A New Look at Leadership (1)

The first work of every leader is to develop a team of like-minded people who will help carry the load of ministry.

Maybe there is no other area in the church where leaders are more likely to get off track than this one: *developing teams of leaders to assist them.* Most pastors spend their time preparing sermons, counseling folks, attending business meetings and visiting the sick. This is wrong!

According to the apostle Paul, the first work of a leader is to *equip* God's people so *they* can perform the work of building up the church (Ephesians 4:11-13)! When a pastor thinks he can do this work by himself, or from the pulpit, or with a dedicated staff, he is terribly mistaken.

Jesus never made leaders that way, and we can't either. Therefore, every leader must handpick a group of people he will *train* for six to twelve months, or until they are capable of doing much of what he does. This means teachers must train teachers, apostles must train missionaries, evangelists must train soulwinners, pastors must train care-givers. And so on. There simply is no substitute for leaders multiplying their work by training others to assist them! Do all of your church leaders follow this wise priority?

A Personal Application

Possibly the most critical passage dealing with leadership and the duty to develop ministers in every church is found in Ephesians 4:11-16. Does your church have the kinds of leaders listed here? Do your leaders raise up new leaders? How can your church improve?

_____
_____
_____
_____
_____
_____
_____
_____
_____
_____
_____
_____
_____
_____
_____
_____

WEEK SEVENTEEN - Day 2

A New Look at Leadership (2)

Solo ministries are normally out of balance and shallow. What every church needs is team ministry.

Jesus worked with the Twelve. The Twelve worked in pairs. Then, Jesus worked with the seventy-two, and they in turn worked in pairs. Peter and John ministered together. Barnabas and Saul worked as a team. Paul also worked with Silas, Timothy, Mark, Aquila, Priscilla, Erastus, Luke and others.

Everywhere you look in the New Testament, leaders worked in teams with other gifted leaders. There are no solo ministries or Board-run ministries in the early church! The implications of these facts are enormous.

If a church leader has the gift of "pastor," then he should immediately begin to pray for a part-time or full-time "evangelist" to join his church team. Next, they should pray for a gifted "leader" and "administrator" to link up with them. They should continue this pursuit until all of the leadership gifts are operating in their church. Working together in humility and unity, these gifted men will provide the church with an incredible degree of balance, depth and ministry!

Is your church praying for and looking to employ this sort of diversified leadership team? Honestly, who leads your church?

A Personal Application

Read Ephesians 4:11-13; Acts 13:1-3 and 14:21-28. Whom has God gifted to lead His church? How do churches sometimes substitute their own ideas for church leaders? Do you think God's leadership plans might be better than our own leadership ideas?

_____
_____
_____
_____
_____
_____
_____
_____
_____
_____
_____
_____
_____
_____
_____

WEEK SEVENTEEN - Day 3

A New Look at Leadership (3)

Successful leaders must be accompanied by submissive followers.

There is a fundamental rule about leadership that Christians too often fail to recognize: *leaders, by definition, have the authority to lead, and followers have the responsibility to follow.*

The instant a leader is not permitted to make leadership decisions, he ceases to be a leader. No congregation has the God-given right to oversee the church's leaders. Instead, the leaders oversee them. However, if a leader gets out of line, then the leadership team must exercise an appropriate measure of discipline — no leader is ever above God's law or church discipline!

The CHURCHMAN FOR GOD has a deep respect in his heart for the principles of authority and submission. He prays for his leaders to be wise, humble, bold and approachable. Additionally, he is prompt to honor the leaders in his church, and he is glad to serve at their side.

Finally, the CHURCHMAN FOR GOD understands that the unity, success and joy of his church depends on the mutual respect of leaders and followers. He knows that they must work together; they must be a team that continually seeks God's best for each other!

A Personal Application

Explain how your church does (or does not) follow these passages on leadership: Hebrews 13:17 and 1 Timothy 5:17-22.

WEEK SEVENTEEN - Day 4

The Qualities of a Good Churchman

It is the privilege of every man of God to serve the Lord by serving His Church.

In every church there are lazy souls — they do as *little* as possible. But the CHURCHMAN FOR GOD is different — he does *as much* as possible. He is not afraid of work; he welcomes it.

When a man gives his heart to the Lord, at that same moment he is expected to give his life to the church as well. So, from the time of his conversion, a man is to be eager to help any way he can.

Some of his works will require humility from him; other works will bestow honor upon him. But whether the labor is noticed by no one or by everyone, the CHURCHMAN FOR GOD delights in knowing he can say "Thank you" to the Lord Jesus Christ by serving in His church.

Don't wait for someone to ask for your help. Whenever there is a need, go to the front of the work-line. Notice needs and invest yourself in meeting them. Be known as someone who can be relied on to do anything you can to make your church a success.

Be a worker!

A Personal Application

Read 1 Corinthians 16:15-18 and Revelation 22:12. How should you highly esteem God's good workers? Who are among the best workers for Christ you know?

WEEK SEVENTEEN - Day 5

The Wrap-Up

If the commitment of every church member paralleled your own commitment, how strong would the church be?

There is no perfect church. Actually, most of them are quite imperfect. But in every good church there are genuine CHURCHMEN FOR GOD who take both the Lord and His Church seriously. They make mistakes along the way, but they usually stumble forward, and in spite of themselves they make a difference — an everlasting difference in people's lives.

Now is the time for you to settle this fact down deep inside of your heart: *Jesus Christ wants me to be one of his special churchmen. He wants me to help people, both temporally and everlastingly. He wants me to impact people for good and for God.*

And there is more. The Lord Jesus Christ also wants to give you special abilities (spiritual gifts) and supernatural resources so your labors will make a difference. In other words, He wants to work with you, at your side, as you serve others. Working together, as a team, the Lord wants to use you to build his Church and expand God's Kingdom!

Have you accepted the Lord's invitation?

A Personal Application

After you read Romans 12:1-11, ask God to show you some specific things He would like you to do. Write out your assignments below.

_____
_____
_____
_____
_____
_____
_____
_____
_____
_____
_____
_____
_____
_____
_____
_____
_____
_____
_____
_____

WEEK SEVENTEEN - Days 6-7

Thinking It Through

Take two days to review the previous five lessons. Write out a prayer that reflects what you desire to apply from these lessons.

What it Means to be
A WITNESS FOR GOD

WEEK EIGHTEEN - Day 1

Born Again

Jesus left heaven to come to earth so men could leave earth and go to heaven!

Men of the world have ten thousand opinions about the route that will take them to heaven. WITNESSES FOR GOD have a single opinion: *they know that they must be born again.*

Every man who experiences a *natural* birth is unqualified for entrance into heaven because his sinful nature rules his heart. He needs a miracle — a heart transplant — if he is going to make it to heaven. And that is why Jesus came to earth — to give people a new heart, a new birth.

Honestly, the majority of men are too proud, independent and unteachable to come to Jesus for a new birth. They want to figure things out for themselves. They want to do things their own way. Frankly, it is precisely this overly inflated self-confident disposition that will keeps most men out of heaven! Let us be frank: *men do not go to heaven because they are "good" or hard working or charitable; they go to heaven because they are truly born again!*

What about you? Can you point to a specific time when Jesus Christ forgave you of all your sins and you pledged your allegiance to him? Are you genuinely born again?

A Personal Application

Based on John 3:1-21, who does and who does not make it into heaven? How should these verses impact your own life?

_____
_____
_____
_____
_____
_____
_____
_____
_____
_____
_____
_____
_____
_____
_____
_____
_____
_____

WEEK EIGHTEEN - Day 2

Heaven is not located at the peak of a mountain with many trails leading to it. There is only ONE way to heaven.

This is a hard, but very true fact: *If Jesus did not come to earth to save sinners from the consequences of their sins, then you and I are still living in our sins, and we are in a huge heap of trouble!*

If Jesus did not come to save us, then we are not saved, our sins are not forgiven, and we are not going to make it to heaven — period. Absolutely *everything* depends on Jesus!

Fortunately, Jesus *did* come to planet earth with the mission of saving people from God's judgment. And more than that, he is the *only* person in the whole world who can do that very thing. Buddha cannot save sinners. Muhammad cannot save sinners. Confucius cannot save sinners. Even Billy Graham cannot save a single sinner. *Only Jesus Christ can rescue sinners!*

Trying to be good will not save you. Attending church will not save you. Giving your money away will not save you. Only Jesus can save you, and he does that when you are prepared to do two things: (1) turn away from your will, and (2) turn toward God's will.

How convinced are you that you are incapable of saving yourself? And how confident are you that Jesus alone can save you from God's everlasting judgment?

A Personal Application

Read John 14:6 and Acts 4:1-12. According to these verses, how many ways are there to get into heaven when you die?

_____
_____
_____
_____
_____
_____
_____
_____
_____
_____
_____
_____
_____
_____
_____
_____
_____
_____
_____

WEEK EIGHTEEN - Day 3

Going to heaven is not automatic. Reservations are required!

Most men will not make it to heaven because they think too lowly of God's standards and too highly of their own character. They are doubly deceived. They are blind to the true nature of God's justice; and they are equally blind to the true nature of their own guilt. (Read this entire paragraph one more time. Meditate on the core natures of God and people.)

Men of the world see things however they want to see them — usually in their own favor. On the other hand, WITNESSES FOR GOD see things as God sees them — always in His favor.

It isn't enough to "feel" safe. And it isn't wise to "take your own chances." Humble men open their hearts and ask the Lord to lead them. They want to know for sure how to deal with their corrupt desires, thoughts, words and actions. They want to understand in simple clear terms how they can overcome the consequences for their sins. They don't want to wait until they die to see if they made the right decisions. They want to know in advance.

Thankfully, that's precisely why God sent Jesus and gave us the Bible — to prepare us for a guaranteed place in heaven!

A Personal Application

Very slowly and prayerfully read this all-important passage: Ephesians 2:1-10. Itemize how many things you learn here about man's lostness and his only hope.

_____
_____
_____
_____
_____
_____
_____
_____
_____
_____
_____
_____
_____
_____
_____
_____
_____
_____

WEEK EIGHTEEN - Day 4

The Roman Road

No man will ever be rescued from his sins until he first acknowledges he is drowning in them.

In the book of Romans the apostle Paul tells us four steps we must take in order to secure a right standing with God. When you read through this list, think of specific people you know who need to become familiar with it.

- First, we must acknowledge that sin is a real part of our personal life: our desires, thoughts, speech and decisions (Romans 3:23).

- Second, we must accept responsibility for our sins and admit that we deserve condemnation, everlasting death, hell (Romans 6:23). This can only happen when we are able to see our sins and self-righteousness as God sees them.

- Third, we must see Jesus dying in our place, accepting the punishment we should have received for our own sins (Romans 5:8).

- Fourth, we must surrender our hearts to Jesus as the Lord and best Friend a sinner could ever have (Romans 10:9-13).

A Personal Application

Read the Roman Road for yourself. Sit and soak on each passages. How could you use these verses to help others? See Romans 3:23; 6:23; 5:8 and 10:9-13.

_____
_____
_____
_____
_____
_____
_____
_____
_____
_____
_____
_____
_____
_____
_____
_____
_____
_____
_____
_____

WEEK EIGHTEEN - Day 5

The Sinner's Prayer

Prayer in itself will never save a sinner, but neither can a sinner be saved without a prayer.

There is only one perfect sinner's prayer: the one that a humble man prays from his heart. It isn't the eloquence of the prayer or the length of the prayer that makes it acceptable to God. A true sinner's prayer simply contains a genuine desire for forgiveness and a sincere motive to follow hard after heaven's will.

Any man may pray any prayer, but that does not automatically mean God listens to his words. It may actually be the case that the majority of all prayers go unheard by God! The Bible says, "God does not hear sinners" (John 9:31).

The Lord looks at the heart, not the words. He wants to see truth, humility and openness. When He finds that, He listens, He hears and He answers.

When a sinner lifts his dirty heart to heaven and asks for cleansing, and when a sinner opens his stubborn will to follow the Lord wherever He leads, that prayer is heard, and that sinner starts his journey as a MAN OF GOD!

Have you prayed this prayer? Have you helped others pray it? Explain.

A Personal Application

What can you learn about a genuine sinner's prayer based on Jesus' words in Luke 18:9-14?

_____
_____
_____
_____
_____
_____
_____
_____
_____
_____
_____
_____
_____
_____
_____
_____
_____
_____
_____
_____

WEEK EIGHTEEN - Days 6-7

Thinking It Through

Take two days to review the previous five lessons. Write out a prayer that reflects what you desire to apply from these lessons.

WEEK NINETEEN - Day 1

The Mission

If it is the mission of Jesus to rescue souls (and it is!), then it must be a man's mission to do the same thing.

God does not measure a man's life by how much he knows, by how much he earns, or by how much people like him. God has a higher standard. He measures men by how much they desire the things that He himself desires! (Re-read and underline this final sentence.)

MEN OF THE WORLD love the things of the world, but WITNESSES FOR GOD love the things of God. Therefore, it is a man's primary duty and privilege to discover those things that are on God's heart, then to make them the main issues of his own heart. It is not difficult to find out what is uppermost in God's interests: *it is souls!*

Jesus did not come into this world to get a job, get a wife, get a family, get lots of possessions, and then retire in some warm resort by the sea. Not for a second! Jesus came to earth to save sinners. That was his mission. That was his heart. And no one today can become a true WITNESS FOR GOD until this is a serious part of his own mission and heart as well.

Is leading people to Christ, salvation and heaven a priority in your life?

A Personal Application

Read Luke 19:1-10, and look inside Jesus' heart. What was (and is) his passion? Why should this mission be important to you?

WEEK NINETEEN - Day 2

An Old Woman on a Lonely Road

If your heart is right, God will use you, regardless of who or where you are.

Donna was an unusual woman. She lived in the backwoods of Kentucky. Neighbors on her lightly traveled road lived far apart, and they rarely talked. As an older woman, she spent her days at home without a husband and without a job. But she did not live without a heart-felt mission.

Donna possessed a strong desire to win people to Christ. Considering her circumstances, it seemed like an impossible dream. But she prayed, and she believed that the Lord would use her. One day a traveling salesman knocked on her door. He wanted to introduce her to "the perfect" vacuum cleaner. She gladly invited him in and listened patiently to everything he had to say. Then she asked him if he would please listen to her for a moment. Donna explained how she loved the Lord Jesus Christ because of all the things he had done for her. With tears and gentle passion, she told the salesman of his own need for a clean heart. That day she led her guest to salvation in Christ!

After a prayer for salvation, the salesman asked her if she had ever lead another person to Christ. "Yes," she said. "You're number twenty-nine!"

A Personal Application

Write out everything you discover about reaching people in impossible places from Acts 8:26-40. Make it personal.

WEEK NINETEEN - Day 3

The Great Commission (1)

From early childhood until late adulthood we should seek to reach souls for Christ.

Jesus finished his ministry on earth where he started it: concerned with the destiny of souls. In the beginning we see Jesus inviting men to follow him so they could learn how to fish for other men (Mk. 1:17). In the end we see Jesus calling on all believers to go throughout the world in order to make disciples of heaven (Matt. 28:19-20).

It's thought provoking . . . Jesus did not invite people to come together for a Sunday morning service between ten and noon, then send them home for a week. Never! Instead, he *taught and trained* people every day of the week. He not only explained the gospel of the Kingdom to people everywhere, he expected these people to spread this gospel everywhere they went as well.

Jesus' mission was not intended solely to give people comfort, but convictions and a strong sense of responsibility to communicate the truth that came out of heaven. He came to create a "domino effect," where one changed person would desire to be used to change another person until the whole world was reached. Jesus looked for men, and when he found them, he worked with them until they became fishers of men.

Can you say, "Train me!"?

A Personal Application

Prepare a list of at least three important points worth remembering regarding the Great Commission in Mark 16:9-20.

_____
_____
_____
_____
_____
_____
_____
_____
_____
_____
_____
_____
_____
_____
_____
_____
_____
_____
_____
_____

WEEK NINETEEN - Day 4

The Great Commission (2)

There is a wandering in every man's heart until he is guided by the Lord's Great Commission.

There are two major components in The Great Commission: *evangelism* and *edification*. Just prior to Jesus' ascension back to heaven, he said this: "Go make disciples of all nations, baptizing them . . ." This is the work of *evangelism* (converting people to the gospel). Jesus also said, "teach them to obey everything I commanded." This is the work of *edification* (converting people to a lifestyle of obedience).

Taken together, this is our Lord's Great Commission: *evangelism* and *edification*. Every church and every Christian should be preeminently occupied with these two responsibilities.

- Does your heart long to be trained so you can be used in evangelism and edification?

- Does your heart desire to be trained so you can live day by day in spiritual obedience?

- Is your church strongly devoted to the works of evangelism and edification? Does it have leaders appointed to oversee these tasks? Are they successful?

A Personal Application

Read Matthew's account of the Great Commission in 28:18-20. Read it slowly and prayerfully. What are the commands in this passage? Are you obeying them?

_____
_____
_____
_____
_____
_____
_____
_____
_____
_____
_____
_____
_____
_____
_____
_____
_____

WEEK NINETEEN - Day 5

Never Say, "I Can't"

Obstacles can be opportunities.

A few years ago, in the country of New Zealand there was a woman who unexpectedly had to go to the hospital because of a horrible infection in her feet. Soon the disease spread to her hands and forearms. There was only one thing the doctors could do to stop the advance of the disease and save her life: she would have to undergo the amputation of both legs and both arms!

For a full year after surgery, this Christian woman suffered from a dreadful depression. Then, one day everything changed. Instead of feeling helpless and sorry for herself, she asked the Lord for an impossible request: *she asked Him to use her!* As she prayed, an idea came to her. She thought if someone would build a box for her body and position it at the right angle, she could learn to write by having a pencil placed in her mouth.

It wasn't easy. But with prayer and a strong determination to witness, she starting writing letters — hundreds upon hundreds of them! She wrote to everyone she knew, then to hundreds of strangers. She told them her story, and she invited them to receive Christ as their Lord and Savior. By the time of her death, she received nearly 1,500 responses from people who told her that they were now Christians because of her life! Never say, "I can't."

A Personal Application

Based on Philippians 1:12-30, how can you overcome your circumstances?

_____
_____
_____
_____
_____
_____
_____
_____
_____
_____
_____
_____
_____
_____
_____
_____
_____
_____
_____
_____
_____

WEEK NINETEEN - Days 6-7

Thinking It Through

Take two days to review the previous five lessons. Write out a prayer that reflects what you desire to apply from these lessons.

WEEK TWENTY - Day 1

Witnessing Power

There will not be a powerful wave of witnessing until there is a powerful filling of the Holy Spirit.

If the act of witnessing were easy, probably every Christian would do it regularly. But the fact is that few Christians witness for Christ because they are afraid. Often would-be witnesses are afraid because they feel inadequate; they don't know what to say. Other potential witnesses are afraid of what people will think if they do speak up for the Kingdom of God and salvation.

Less than 5% of all believers ever lead another person to Christ because they are paralyzed by some form of fear!

According to Jesus, it takes a special power from the Holy Spirit to become an effective witness — it takes help from above. With this special power-to-witness gifting, Christians overcome their fear of talking to people about spiritual matters. Without this enablement, Christians turn into wimps who have a bad case of "the cat's got your tongue."

Starting today, pray for witnessing power — the power you need to tell people about the things of God. You may never become an evangelist, but you *can* become someone who cares about people's souls. And you *can* help people find the path to heaven! Ask God for His help!

A Personal Application

Read Acts 1:1-8, and ask the Lord for the power you need to witness. Write out your prayer below.

_____
_____
_____
_____
_____
_____
_____
_____
_____
_____
_____
_____
_____
_____
_____
_____
_____
_____
_____
_____

WEEK TWENTY - Day 2

Changed People Change People

Only a man who personally knows God's forgiveness can help other men find God's grace.

The most effective witnessing comes from people who know from their own experience what it means to be forgiven, to be baptized, to trust Christ completely and to follow the Lord moment by moment. More often than not, the Lord uses changed people to change people.

Is your heart up to date with the Lord? Do you have a testimony (a personal experience with Jesus) that has impacted your life?

If the answer to these questions is "Yes," then you can be a witness for Christ. But if the answer is, "No," or "I'm not sure," then you need to go to "square one." You need to kneel . . . envision the cross with Christ dying for your sins . . . stare in his face and humbly ask for complete forgiveness for every sin you have ever committed. When you do this, when you *know* that the connection has taken place, you will then have a testimony that everyone will need to hear!

Whatever else you may do in life, get a salvation testimony! Do you have one? Do you share it with others so they might get one as well?

A Personal Application

Read the salvation testimony of Paul in Acts 9:1-18. Then write out your own testimony in the space below. Describe your life before, at, and after conversion.

WEEK TWENTY - Day 3

Being a Star in Darkness

Witnessing is a work of the heart, mind and will; it is full of emotion, reason and volition.

In a complete witnessing experience you will have the opportunity to do more than share your *testimony*, you will also have the privilege of sharing God's *truth*. Conversion to Christ involves more than spiritual *inspiration*, there is Scriptural *information* to understand and respond to as well.

The Bible describes people who witness to others with the aid of God's Word as "stars." *That could be you!* Every time you explain to someone a message from the Bible, you are a bright star to them — like the North Star! As they listen to you describe God's plan of salvation, light and clarity are entering their darkness and overcoming their misunderstandings.

In this book you will soon discover the essential Biblical truths a person needs to know in order to make it to heaven. Meanwhile, ask the Lord to make crystal clear to you His message of salvation. It is next to impossible to lead others into a confident relationship with God if your own confidence is weak. Therefore, you must determine that you will not only *know* God's forgiveness, you will also know how to *explain* God's plan of salvation to others!

A Personal Application

How does the Bible describe a witness in Philippians 2:12-16? How can you personalize this message?

_____
_____
_____
_____
_____
_____
_____
_____
_____
_____
_____
_____
_____
_____
_____
_____
_____
_____
_____
_____
_____
_____
_____

WEEK TWENTY - Day 4

The Great Exchange Explained

Good Friday is "good" because God made an exchange possible on that day of our sins for Jesus' righteousness!

If people knew how good Jesus is and how bad we humans are, there would be a great deal more prayer for forgiveness and salvation. But, unfortunately, we are often too self-righteous to ask for God's help. We willfully forget that no one will ever make it to heaven on the basis of his or her character. We vainly imagine that God is only love, and that He will overlook our setting Him aside in order to do whatever we want. But we are mistaken. God is also holy and just. Therefore He will hold each one of us accountable for all of our desires, thoughts, words and decisions! And that means we're in trouble, unless Jesus helps us!

When Jesus hung on the cross, God the Father took all of the sins of everyone from the beginning of time and placed them on Christ. At that moment, he became our Substitute, dying in our place and paying the price we should have paid for our sins! And God did more. *He offered an exchange: our sins in exchange for Jesus' righteousness (or right standing with God).* From that time forward, everyone who would come to God through the merits of Jesus Christ would be forgiven and adopted into His everlasting family! Unquestionably, this is the most remarkable reality in the whole world!

A Personal Application

Prayerfully read 2 Corinthians 5:11-21. Take your time. Underline every key word and phrase. Then explain both the "message" and the "ministry" of reconciliation.

WEEK TWENTY - Day 5

The Great Exchange Pictured

When you witness, you can do more than TELL the salvation story, you can SHOW it as well.

Examine "The Great Exchange" diagram below until you can reproduce it from memory. Envision yourself explaining this drawing with someone who needs Christ.

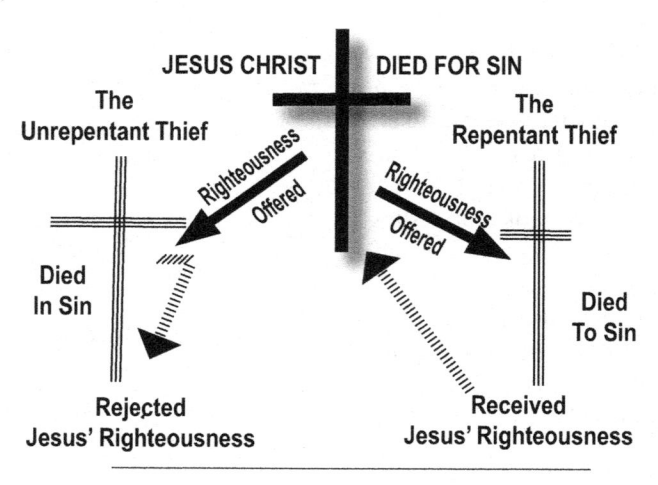

JESUS CHRIST | DIED FOR SIN

The Unrepentant Thief — Righteousness Offered — Died In Sin — Rejected Jesus' Righteousness

The Repentant Thief — Righteousness Offered — Died To Sin — Received Jesus' Righteousness

A Personal Application

The Great Exchange is explained in these passages: 2 Corinthians 5:17-21 and Isaiah 52:13-53:15. Have these verses become your own experience? Explain.

_____
_____
_____
_____
_____

WEEK TWENTY - Days 6-7

Thinking It Through

Take two days to review the previous five lessons. Write out a prayer that reflects what you desire to apply from these lessons.

WEEK TWENTY-ONE - Day 1

The Bridge to Heaven Explained

Our personal sins have destroyed the only bridge to heaven, but God's grace has reconstructed it!

In our pride it is easy for us to imagine that we can make it to heaven by our own ideas and efforts. We assume that God is too loving to send anyone to a literal hell and that we are too good to be actually condemned. But this faulty thinking is doubly wrong: (1) we are not nearly as guiltless as we assume, and (2) while God's love provides an escape from hell, it does not eliminate its reality or severity!

Therefore, the most important thing a man will ever do is bow his heart before God, acknowledge the ugliness of his sins, turn from them as fully as possible, and pledge his grateful loyalty to the Lord Jesus Christ for the gift of everlasting salvation. The second most important thing he will ever do is help others come to know mankind's only Savior — Jesus Christ.

The WITNESS FOR GOD understands that Jesus Christ is God's "bridge" over the canyon that separates us from salvation. He knows that no one can get to the other side (to the land of heaven) without that "bridge." So, the WITNESS FOR GOD tells people his personal testimony as well as the story of why Jesus came to earth so we could go to heaven!

A Personal Application

What does Peter have to say to people about Jesus and salvation? See Acts 2:36-47.

WEEK TWENTY-ONE - Day 2

The Bridge to Heaven Pictured

There is an impassable gap between every sinner and God; there is a bridge, too!

Study this easy chart until you can draw it from memory. Think through how you will tell someone the gospel story as you draw this powerful image.

YOU ON EARTH		GOD IN HEAVEN
Substituting God for gods		Perfect Holiness
Idolizing people & things		Perfect Love
Misusing God's name	D	Perfect Truth
Dishonoring the Sabbath	E	Perfect Obedience
Disobeying parents	A	Perfect Humility
Hating and killing people	T	Perfect Desires
Sexual immorality	H	Perfect Thoughts
Stealing		Perfect Speech
Telling lies		Perfect Decisions
Coveting		Perfect Everything
	HELL	

A Personal Application

Read Romans 7:14-25, and explain how the "bridge" to heaven has impacted your life.

_____
_____
_____
_____
_____

WEEK TWENTY-ONE - Day 3

The Roman Road (again)

The best way to find heaven is to study God's own directions for getting there!

We discussed this subject earlier, but it is so critical, it is worth going over it again.

In addition to telling people your testimony and showing them the gospel with drawings, you also need to be able to explain to people God's plan of salvation from the Bible. And the easiest way to do that is to work your way through six verses from the Book of Romans.

Open your Bible to the very first blank page. Write these words there: **THE ROMAN ROAD - Romans 3:23.** In case you forget where to begin, this page will always remind you of the starting point. Then turn to this passage, and put a circle around the number "23," or underline the verse. At the side of this verse, write: "6:23." This will be your next passage. Go there and mark it. Do the same thing with 5:8 and 10:9-13.

Now, study these verses until you know them inside-out. Be certain that your own experience corresponds with these words. Think of ways to *explain* and *illustrate* each of these passages. Rehearse them in your mind. Go over them, again and again.

A Personal Application

In the space below write out a brief illustration you can use when you explain each point in "The Roman Road."

WEEK TWENTY-ONE - Day 4

Being Ready

Heaven is filled with people who responded to the gospel because someone prepared himself and then shared the message with others.

The only reason you are on your way to heaven is because someone took the time to tell you how to get there! And that means they had to prepare themselves first. Then, when they were ready, they told you (and probably others) the Good News about Jesus Christ and personal salvation.

If you are a Christian, you are in debt to some witness . . . to someone who kindly and boldly told you how you could find heaven. This is true for every Christian. No one gets to heaven without directions, and no one finds these directions without someone pointing the way, especially through a testimony and a teaching.

If there were any room for a single regret in heaven, it would be this: *I wish I had introduced more of my friends, and even strangers, to Jesus Christ!* Don't let this happen to you. Prepare yourself so you can make a difference in someone's destiny. Take people with you to heaven!

Who is there you know who needs Jesus Christ and salvation?

A Personal Application

What specific points does Peter make about being ready to witness? See 1 Peter 3:1-17.

WEEK TWENTY-ONE - Day 5

Sharing the Gospel

Witnessing is not a one or two or three-time experience; it is a lifestyle. You should always be prepared to share.

Today, will be your special opportunity to tell someone what you have learned about *The Roman Road* or *The Bridge to Life* or *The Great Exchange*. Pray for a divine appointment. Then, write out the results of your experience below.

_____
_____
_____
_____
_____
_____
_____
_____
_____
_____
_____
_____
_____
_____
_____
_____
_____
_____
_____
_____
_____
_____

WEEK TWENTY-ONE - Days 6-7

Thinking It Through

Take two days to review the previous five lessons. Write out a prayer that reflects what you desire to apply from these lessons.

Made in the USA
Middletown, DE
29 June 2019